For Georgio,
in memory to Your 70th birthday
You celebrate in Germany!
Our best whishes for You!

Hermann Josef + Katharina
DUPONT

10. Sept 2008

TRIER

Die mittelalterliche Stadt in Bildern
The Medieval City in Pictures

Text und Zeichnungen von Lambert Dahm
Texts and Drawings by Lambert Dahm

Verlag edition treverorum der H&S Virtuelle Welten Trier 2004

Vorwort
Foreword

Das mittelalterliche Trier begegnet uns im Stadtbild auf Schritt und Tritt. Im Gegensatz zu den wenigen überirdischen Zeugnissen des römischen Triers erscheint es uns verständlicher, weil besser erhalten und funktional klarer. Aber ist es das auch? Ich glaube: nein - und so dachte wohl auch Lambert Dahm, dessen beeindruckende Zeichnungen des mittelalterlichen Triers in dieser Publikation zu sehen sind. Sein Ziel war es, ein lebendiges, verdichtetes Gesamtbild der mittelalterlichen Stadt zu schaffen. Dies ist ihm auf seine einzigartige Weise gelungen. Die aufwendigen Zeichnungen nehmen uns mit auf eine über 1000-jährige Reise durch das nachantike, mittelalterliche Trier. Lambert Dahm war jahrzehntelang am Rheinischen Landesmuseum Trier als Museumszeichner tätig. Seine Zeichnungen sind von den Erfahrungen seiner engagierten Arbeit geprägt und bestechen durch ihren Detailreichtum. Seine leicht verständlichen Texte laden ein, Einblicke in den geschichtlichen Hintergrund zu gewinnen. Ergänzt werden Lambert Dahms Zeichnungen durch beeindruckende Fotos von Fundstücken und aktuelle Aufnahmen der Stadt. Aufbauend auf dem vor einem Jahr präsentierten Band "Trier - Die römische Stadt in Bildern" kann der Betrachter nun also 2000 Jahre Stadtgeschichte Revue passieren lassen. Ob Laie, Fachmann oder passionierter Stadtliebhaber: Diese Publikation möchte Sie alle gleichermaßen einladen, den Reiz und die Lebendigkeit der Stadt der Kurfürsten, Bischöfe und Bürger zu entdecken.

Ich wünsche Ihnen viel Vergnügen bei der Lektüre.

Jörg Henerichs
Herausgeber

We encounter medieval Trier at even turn in the cityscape. In contrast to the few manifestations of Roman Trier visible above ground, the medieval appears more familiar to us because we see so many of these buildings in their functional entirety. But is that true? I do not believe it is, nor does Lambert Dahm, whose impressive drawings of medieval Trier can be seen in this publication. His goal was to create a dense, vivid picture of the medieval city in its totality. He has succeeded in his own distinct way. The detailed drawings take us on a 1000-year journey through post-Roman and medieval Trier. His drawings are distinguished by his experience during his long years of dedicated work as the draftsman in the Roman Archaeological Museum and captivate the observer with their rich detail. His easily understood texts invite us to gain an insight into the historical background. Lambert Dahm's drawings are supplemented by attractive photos of finds and pictures of the modern city. Starting with the book Trier, The Roman City in Pictures, presented in 2003, 2000 years of history can now pass in review. This publication would like to invite all equally - whether amateur, expert, or Trier enthusiast - to discover the charm and the vitality of the city of Electors, Bishops, and townspeople.

I wish everyone much pleasure in reading this book.

Jörg Henerichs
Publisher

Inhalt — Table of Contents

Geschichtlicher Überblick - Zur Entwicklung der Stadt
Historical Overview - The Development of the City

Das frühe Mittelalter.

So reich die Stadt Trier an Funden und Bauten aus römischer Zeit ist, so gering sind die Zeugnisse aus dem frühen Mittelalter, sieht man einmal von dem Weitergebrauch und der Umnutzung antiker Anlagen ab. Nach der Verlegung des Kaiserhofes des röm. Westreiches von Trier nach Mailand und dem Umzug der Präfektur nach Arles, etwa zwischen 392 und 407, verlor Trier seine staatspolitische Bedeutung und wohl auch einen Teil seiner Einwohnerschaft, blieb aber weiterhin Zentrum der Provinz Belgica prima und ein Schwerpunkt des frühen Christentums, mit dem ältesten Bischofssitz auf deutschem Boden.

Für den zeitlichen Beginn des frühen Mittelalters werden in der Forschung zwei verschiedene Zeitpunkte gesehen, bevorzugt entweder der Beginn der Völkerwanderung etwa ab 375 n. Chr. oder aber die Absetzung des letzten Kaisers des Westreiches, Romulus Augustulus, 476 n. Chr.

Nach den Wirren durch die häufigen Germaneneinfälle in der ersten Hälfte des 5. Jhs. erlebte Trier nach der Mitte des Jahrhunderts wahrscheinlich eine relativ ruhige Zeit. Diese verdankten Stadt und Umland wohl dem römischen Statthalter fränkischer Herkunft, dem Comes (Graf) Arbogast. Als Christ, er soll später gar Bischof geworden sein, war ihm wohl der Erhalt der in hohem Ansehen stehenden Trierer Christengemeinde mit dem Bischof an der Spitze angelegen, da sie ein Ruhepol innerhalb der instabilen Gesellschaft war und als einzige Institution den Untergang des römischen Imperiums überlebte. Arbogast dürfte die Verantwortung für das wohl noch römisch verfaßte Gemeinwesen bis etwa 477 getragen haben, ehe dann auch Trier um 485 in das Rheinische Frankenland einbezogen wurde. Wenig später, zu Beginn des 6. Jhs., gliederte der aus dem Geschlecht der Merowinger stammende Frankenkönig Chlodwig (481-511) auch dieses Land in sein Gesamtfrankenreich ein. Trier zeigte zu dieser Zeit noch seine alten Strukturen der Römerstadt.

Es ist wohl der Autorität des Bischofs zu verdanken, daß Stadt und Umland nicht von einer totalen Anarchie erfaßt wurden. Der Bischof war, gleich dem König, Rechtsnachfolger des Reiches, wodurch der zuvor von der Kirche genutzte Staatsbesitz nunmehr Kirchenbesitz wurde. Waren es zur Römerzeit die Staatsbauten, welche das Stadtbild bestimmten, so waren es später die Kirchen und Klosteranlagen, die den Charakter der Stadt dominierten.

The Early Middle Ages

As rich as Trier is in finds and structures from the Roman era, it is all the more lacking in evidence from the Early Middle Ages, aside from those ancient structures which have remained in continuous use or were used for other purposes. Following the removal of the Imperial court of the Western Roman Empire from Trier to Milan and the transfer of the prefecture to Arles, somewhere between 392 and 407, Trier lost its political significance and probably also a number of its inhabitants. However, it continued to be the center of the Province of *Belgica prima* and a cornerstone of Early Christianity, with the oldest bishop's see in Germany.

Historical research stipulates two different dates for the beginning of the Early Middle Ages, preferring either the beginning of the tribal migrations of the Germanic people, beginning about AD 375, or the deposing of the last emperor of the Western Empire, Romulus Augustulus in AD 476.

Following the tumult created by the frequent Germanic raids in the first half of the 5th century, Trier most likely experienced a relatively peaceful period after the middle of the century. The city and the entire region no doubt owed this calm after the storm to the Roman governor of Frankish origin, Count (Latin *comes*) Arbogast. As a Christian, he is said to have even become bishop later on. To be sure, preserving the highly respected Christian community with its bishop as leader was of significance to him, as it represented tranquility within the unstable society and as this community had remained the sole surviving institution in the downfall of the Roman Empire. Most likely until about 477, Arbogast bore responsibility for the community no doubt still living under Roman regulations; but then Trier as well was incorporated into the Frankish lands of the Rhine region. A bit later, at the beginning of the 6th century, the Frankish King Clovis (481-511) of the Merovingian clan integrated this region into his Kingdom of the Franks. At this time, Trier retained its old structures from the Roman city.

Owing to the authority of the bishop, the city and the region did not fall into total anarchy. Like the king, the bishop was the legal successor of the Empire, and thus state property formerly used by the Church henceforth became Church property. Whereas government buildings had determined the cityscape in the Roman era, it was later the churches, monasteries, and convents that dominated the character of the city.

Die Franken, sie hatten im Gegensatz zu den meisten übrigen Germanenstämmen den katholischen Glauben römischer Form angenommen, bauten ihre Reichsordnung im wesentlichen nach römischem Vorbild auf und ließen dabei die Stellung des Bischofs unangetastet. Trier wurde Sitz eines fränkischen Gaugrafen (Comes), des Statthalters des fränkischen Königs im Trier-Gau. Seinen Sitz soll der Gaugraf im Bereich der Kaiseraula (Basilika) genommen haben.

Nach dem Tod König Chlodwigs 511 teilten seine Söhne das Reich. Theuderich I. (511-534) erhielt den größten Teil, zu dem die ehemals römischen Provinzen Germania prima und secunda, die Belgica prima mit Trier sowie ein Teil der Belgica secunda mit Reims gehörten. Dieses Teilreich trug den Namen Austrasien. Trier als Sitz von Bischof und Gaugraf blieb so auch weiterhin Mittelpunkt der Region.

Eine das 6. Jh. in Trier prägende Persönlichkeit war der 526/27 auf das Betreiben Königs Theuderich I. berufene Bischof Nicetius. Nicetius entstammte einer vornehmen gallo-römischen Familie und kam wahrscheinlich aus Aquitanien nach hier, er soll zuvor Abt in Limoges gewesen sein. Einer der größten Verdienste von Bischof Nicetius war der Wiederaufbau des seit Jahrzehnten schwer beschädigten Trierer Doms, seiner Bischofskirche. Ihm ist es auch gelungen, die zuvor gelockerten alten Metropolitanrechte neu zu festigen. Nicetius starb um 566 und wurde seinem Wunsch entsprechend in der Nähe des von ihm hochverehrten hl. Bischof Maximinus auf dem Nordfriedhof bestattet.

Im ausgehenden 6. Jh. ist den Bischöfen eine immer größere Macht zugewachsen, so daß nicht mehr der Gaugraf, sondern der Bischof in Trier gebot. Wohl aus diesem Grund verlegte der Gaugraf im späten 7. Jh. seinen Sitz nach Bitburg. In den sechziger Jahren des 8. Jhs. machte Karl der Große diese Entwicklung wieder rückgängig, die Hoheitsrechte gingen erneut in die Gewalt des Grafen über, mit Ausnahme der bischöflichen Domimmunität und der ihm unterstehenden Einrichtungen.

Das 7. Jh. war u.a. auch das Jahrhundert der Klostergründungen in Trier. Es bestanden allerdings, wie durch Zeitzeugen belegt, bereits seit dem 4. Jh. Mönchsgemeinschaften in Trier. Über ihre weitere Entwicklung bis zum 7. Jh. ist kaum etwas bekannt. Erkennbar ist, daß die wichtigsten Klöster in der Nähe der Gräber der heiligen Trierer Bischöfe, Eucharius im Süden und Maximinus und Paulinus im Norden der Stadt, entstanden sind. Das Kloster St. Maximin gilt als ältestes Kloster auf deutschem Boden.

Die frühen Regeln der Klostergemeinschaften wurden im 7. Jh. weitgehend durch die neue Klosterordnung des Benedikt von Nursia abgelöst. Sie wurden außer von St. Maximin und St. Eucharius auch von den Klöstern St. Martin und St. Maria ad Martyres übernommen. Unter Bischof Modoald wurden die beiden Frauenklöster St. Symphorian und St. Irminen, letzteres im Bereich der römischen Horrea, für weibliche Adelsangehörige gegründet.

In contrast to most of the other Germanic tribes, the Franks, who had adopted the Catholic faith in the Roman form, structured their kingdom essentially according to the Roman model and left the position of the bishop untouched. Trier became the seat of a Frankish *Gaugraf* (Latin *comes*), a district leader, the deputy of the Frankish King in the Trier *Gau* (district). The seat of the *Gaugraf* is said to have been in the vicinity of the Roman Imperial audience hall (present-day "Basilika").

After Clovis died in 511, his sons divided the kingdom. Theuderich I (511-534) received the largest portion, to which belonged the former Roman provinces of *Germania prima* and *secunda*, *Belgica prima* with Trier as well as a section of *Belgica secunda* with Rheims. This section of the kingdom was called *Austrasia*. As the seat of a bishop and a *Gaugraf*, Trier thus remained the center of the region.

One of the influential personalities of the 6th century was Nicetius, who became bishop at the prompting of King Theuderich I in 526/527. Nicetius came from a prominent Gallo-Roman family and moved probably from Aquitaine to Trier; he is said to have been an abbot in Limoges. One of Bishop Nicetius's greatest accomplishments was the renovation of his Bishop's Church, Trier Cathedral, which had stood severely damaged for decades. He also succeeded in solidifying the previously reduced archbishop's rights. Nicetius died around 566 and was buried according to his wishes in the north cemetery near Bishop Maximinus, whom he venerated highly.

The power of the bishops increased greatly towards the end of the 6th century, so that the *Gaugraf* no longer had supreme authority, but rather the bishop. Probably for that reason, the *Gaugraf* moved his seat of power to Bitburg in the late 7th century. In the 760s, Charlemagne reversed this development: the sovereign rights were once again placed in the hands of the *Gaugraf*, with the exception of the area of the Cathedral city and the institutions under the authority of the archbishop.

The 7th century was, among other things, also the century of monastery and convent foundings in Trier. However, as evidence shows, monastic communities had existed as early as the 4th century. Little is known about their further development up to the 7th century. Evidence shows that the most important monastic communities arose near the graves of the Trier bishops who were recognized as saints, Eucharius to the south and Maximinus and Paulinus to the north of the city. St. Maximin's is considered the oldest monastery in Germany.

In the 7th century, the early rules of the monastic communities were replaced for the most part by the new monastic rule of Benedict of Nursia, taken over by not only St. Maximin's and St. Eucharius' but also by St. Martin's and St. Maria ad Martyres. Under Bishop Modoald, the two convents St. Symphorian's and St. Irmina's were founded for women of noble birth, the latter convent in the buildings of a former Roman food storehouse.

Etwa zur gleichen Zeit, mit König Dagobert I. (629-639), ging auch die merowingische Dynastie zu Ende. Ihr folgten die Karolinger, deren hervorragendste Persönlichkeit Kaiser Karl d. Gr. war, der das Reich von 768 bis 814 lenkte. In seine Zeit fällt auch die Wiederherstellung der alten Kirchenprovinz Trier mit den Suffraganbistümern Metz, Toul und Verdun. Als Metropoliten führten die Trierer Bischöfe seitdem den Titel Erzbischof. Bauwerke aus dieser Zeit kann Trier nicht aufweisen, ebenso fehlen Zeugnisse für das wirtschaftliche Leben in Trier.

Das Reich litt seit dem Tod König Chlodwigs unter den ständigen Teilungen und Wiedervereinigungen, die sich mehr oder weniger über alle Jahrhunderte hinzogen. Eine der folgenreichsten Teilungen ist die von 843, bei der im Vertrag von Verdun u.a. nach Sprachen getrennt wurde, wodurch praktisch im Westen ein romanisches und im Osten ein germanisches Herrschaftsgebiet entstanden, Grundsteine für die späteren Nationalstaaten Frankreich und Deutschland.

Ein weiteres herausragendes Ereignis des 9. Jhs. war der Einfall der Normannen in der Karwoche 882, bei dem Stadt und Land schwerste Schäden erlitten, hauptsächlich die Klöster wurden gebrandschatzt. Die römischen Großbauten der Stadt überlebten auch diese Katastrophe, aber der durch das quadratische Straßennetz mitgeprägte römische Stadtcharakter ging nun endgültig verloren. Beim folgenden Wiederaufbau der Stadt entstand eine völlig neue Straßenführung, die sich in der Altstadt bis heute weitgehend erhalten hat. Die Straßen führten fast strahlenförmig von der Westseite der Domimmunität zu den wichtigen Punkten der Stadt wie der Moselbrücke, den Klöstern nahe dem Moselufer und den Stadtzugängen.

Im Jahre 895 errichtete König Arnulf (887-899) das Unterkönigreich Lothringen für seinen Sohn Zwentibold, der den Trierer Erzbischof Radbod zum Kanzler berief. Die Nähe zum Königsamt war für die Trierer Bischöfe und Kirche seit dem 6. Jh. von ausschlaggebender Bedeutung. Wie bei den großzügigen Gebietsschenkungen im Hunsrück usw. verzichtete der König nunmehr auf seine Rechte in Trier und dem Trierer Land. Damit entstand ein festes bischöfliches Territorium, der Grundstock für das spätere kurtrierische Territorium.

Das 10 Jh. entwickelte eine neue Bautätigkeit, so wurde im Jahre 934 mit dem Neubau der ottonischen Maximinkirche begonnen, die unter Abt Hugo zügig errichtet wurde, so daß die Osthälfte 942 geweiht werden konnte. Im Jahre 955 weihte Erzbischof Ruotbert (931-956) die wieder hergestellte Südostkirche der alten römischen Kirchenanlage, die am Ort der heutigen Liebfrauenkirche stand. Wenig später gründete Erzbischof Heinrich I. (956-964) westlich der Domimmunität, die immer ein Herzstück der Stadt war, einen Kleinhandelsmarkt, den heutigen Hauptmarkt. Das 958 dort errichtete Marktkreuz war ein Symbol erzbischöflicher Herrschaft sowie des Gottes- und Marktfriedens.

At about the same time, the Merovingian dynasty de facto came to an end with King Dagobert I (629-639). They were followed by the Carolingians, whose most outstanding personality was Charlemagne (768-814). During his reign, the ancient ecclesiastical province of Trier was restored with the suffragan dioceses of Metz, Toul, and Verdun. Restored as Metropolitans, their ancient title, the Trier bishops henceforth bore the title of archbishop. Trier can show no structures from this period, nor are there records of the economic life in Trier.

After the death of King Clovis, the kingdom suffered from constant divisions and reunifications which more or less continued through the centuries. One of the most momentous divisions came about in 843, when the Treaty of Verdun separated not only the languages but created Romanic rule in the West and Germanic rule in the East, the foundations of the later nation states of France and Germany.

A further pivotal event of the 9th century was the invasion of the Vikings during Easter week of 882, when the city and the countryside suffered enormous devastation: it was mainly the monasteries and convents that were burned down. The large Roman structures survived this catastrophe, but the chessboard pattern of streets characterizing the Roman city was irrevocably lost. The following restoration of the city created a completely new street pattern, which has been preserved more or less in the Old City to this day. The streets radiated from the west side of the Cathedral city to the important places in the city, such as the Moselle bridge, the convents and monasteries near the Moselle embankment and to the access points into the city.

In 895, King Arnulf (887-899) established the lesser kingdom of Lothringen (Lorraine) for his son Zwentibold, who named the Trier Archbishop Radbod royal Chancellor. The closeness to the kings had been decisive for the Trier bishops and the Church since the 6th century. Along with the generous bestowal of land in the Hunsruck mountains and elsewhere, the King subsequently relinquished his rights in Trier and the Trier region. Thus a defined episcopal territory was established, the basis for the later Electoral State of Trier.

The 10th century saw the development of fresh building activity; for example, the new Ottonian St. Maximin's Church was begun in 934, quickly constructed under Abbot Hugo, so that the east half could be consecrated in 942. In 955, Archbishop Ruotbert (931-956) consecrated the newly restored southeast church of the old Roman church complex, where the Church of Our Lady stands today. A short time later, Archbishop Henry I (956-964) founded a small market, the present-day Main Market, west of the Cathedral city, a center of the city from early on. The Market Cross erected in 958 was a symbol of the archbishop's rule over the city as well as a symbol of spiritual and secular peace on the marketplace guaranteed by the archbishop.

TRIERER PRÄGUNG 7. JH.

In der nachrömischen Zeit hatte die Stadt ihre städtebauliche Einheit und Geschlossenheit nach und nach verloren. In der Umgebung der römischen Großbauten hatten sich, wie später auch bei den Klöstern, Siedlungen gebildet, die eher dörflichen Charakter zeigten. Mit dem neuen Markt entstand ein neuer wirtschaftlicher Mittelpunkt, der sich zum neuen Stadtzentrum Triers entwickelte. Von hier gingen, wie ja bemerkt, die wichtigsten Straßen der Stadt nach Norden, Süden und Westen (zur Moselbrücke) ab. Auch der Nachfolger Erzbischof Heinrichs I., Erzbischof Dietrich I. (965-977), förderte neben dem Wiederaufbau der Abteien St. Martin und St. Marien insbesondere den Ausbau der Stadt. Er gilt auch als Stifter der neuen Marktkirche, der heutigen Kirche St. Gangolf. Sein Nachfolger, Erzbischof Egbert (977-993), setzte neue Akzente. Als kunstsinniger Mann förderte er insbesondere die Schulen und Werkstätten für Buchmalerei und Goldschmiedekunst in Trier. Die dort entstanden Werke zählen zu den großen und hervorragenden Leistungen der ottonischen Zeit. Seine Neubaumaßnahmen an der Domwestseite kamen leider nicht über die Planung und erste Fundamente hinaus. Sein Nachfolger, Erzbischof Ludolf (994-1008), führte die Arbeiten nicht weiter, er sicherte vielmehr die Domimmunität um das Jahr 1000 durch eine starke Ummauerung. Erst unter Erzbischof Poppo von Babenberg (1016-1047) wurde der Domausbau nach völlig neuen Plänen wieder in Angriff genommen. Es entstand u.a. der gewaltige Domwestbau, wie er heute noch erhalten ist.

Erzbischof Poppo ist auch die Erhaltung der Porta Nigra zu verdanken, die er zu Ehren des hl. Simeon zu einer doppelgeschossigen Kirche ausbauen ließ und so vor dem Untergang als Steinbruch bewahrte. Gleich daneben entstand im Jahre 1037 das Simeonstift, ein Kanonikerstift, dessen noch weitgehend erhaltenes Quadrum als das älteste auf deutschem Boden gilt. Auch die großzügig angelegte Simeonstraße, zwischen Porta Nigra und Hauptmarkt, ist Erzbischof Poppo zu verdanken.

In the post-Roman era, the city had lost its urban structural unity and cohesion little by little. Settlements formed with a village-like character in the vicinity of the large Roman structures, as they did later near the monastic communities. The relocated market created a new economic focal point which developed into Trier's new city center. As mentioned above, the most important city streets radiated to the north, south, and west (to the Moselle bridge). The successor to Archbishop Henry I, Archbishop Dietrich I (965-977), promoted especially the expansion of the city along with the restoration of St. Martin's and St. Mary's abbeys. He is considered the likely founder of the new Market church, the present-day Church of St. Gangolf. His successor, Archbishop Egbert (977-993), set new standards: as a man with artistic tastes, he furthered to a great degree the schools and workshops for book illumination and goldsmith work in Trier. The works of art fashioned there count among the outstanding achievements of the Ottonian period. Unfortunately, his building measures on the west side of the Cathedral did not rise beyond the planning stage and the beginning foundations. Archbishop Ludolf (994-1008), Egbert's successor, did not continue the work; rather he secured the Cathedral city with a strong wall around 1000. Finally, Archbishop Poppo of Babenberg (1016-1047) undertook the Cathedral expansion according to completely new plans, giving rise to the massive west section of the Cathedral still preserved today.

The Porta Nigra owes its continued existence also to Archbishop Poppo, who had the gate converted into a double church in honor of St. Simeon, thus safeguarding it from gradual destruction as a stone quarry. He instituted the neighboring Simeon's Collegiate Foundation in 1037, a college of canons; the largely preserved cloister quadrangle counts as the oldest in Germany. The Archbishop was also responsible for the spaciously laid-out Simeon Street between the Porta Nigra and the Main Market.

EGBERT

POPPO VON BABENBERG

Das Hoch- und Spätmittelalter

Mit dem Beginn der romanischen Zeit, der Zeit um 1000, wurde nicht nur ein Wandel in der Kunst, hier besonders in der Architektur, deutlich, diese Zeit wird auch als Wendepunkt des Denkens angesehen. Es vollzog sich ein Umdenkungsprozeß, der weltanschaulich, politisch und rechtlich von grundlegender Bedeutung war, aber auch zu Spannungen führte.

Mit dem Beginn des 11. Jhs. häuften und verstärkten sich in Trier die Spannungen und der Streit zwischen dem Erzbischof und den verschiedensten Interessengruppen, welche zum Teil groteske Züge annahmen. Mal ging es um die Besetzung des Trierer Bischofsstuhls, mal um die weltlichen Hoheitsrechte des Erzbischofs. Die Stadt wurde im wesentlichen von privilegierten Gruppen wie Adelsgeschlechtern, Angehörigen des Hofes, Ministerialen usw. dominiert und geprägt, sie alle versuchten, ihren Besitz auf Kosten des Erzbischofs zu vergrößern.

Ihre Vormachtstellung drückte sich u.a. in ihren Wehr- und Wohntürmen aus, von welchen u.a. der Frankenturm, die unteren Geschosse des Turmes Jerusalem am Domfreihof und das in dieser Tradition im frühen 13. Jh. entstandene Dreikönigenhaus in der Simeonstraße erhalten blieben.

ALBERO

Aber nicht nur mit den genannten Gruppen kam es zu Streitigkeiten von Seiten des Erzbischofs, sondern auch mit den großen Abteien, hier insbesondere mit St. Maximin, deren Territorien durch Schenkungen usw. weit größer waren als das des späteren Kurstaates. Wie bereits zuvor andere, versuchte auch Erzbischof Albero (1131-1152), die Abtei aus der Reichsunmittelbarkeit zu lösen, um sie seiner Hoheit zu unterstellen, was ihm mit Hilfe König Konrads III. (1138-1153) auch gelang.

Eine für die Stadt wichtige Baumaßnahme war der Bau der Stadtmauer, mit der unter Erzbischof Bruno (1102-1124) begonnen wurde. Diese neue Befestigung verkleinerte das alte Stadtgebiet erheblich, so daß nur noch ein Drittel der römischen Stadtausdehnung blieb. In den folgenden Jahrzehnten formierten sich neue Interessengruppen, die Einfluß auf die Geschehnisse in der Stadt nehmen wollten, was wiederum zu neuen Spannungen führte, die auch im 13. Jahrhundert fortdauerten. Dabei ging es zunächst um die Besetzung des Bischofsamtes.

The High and Late Middle Ages

With the beginning of the Romanesque period, about 1000, a transformation occurred not only, in artistic style which can be seen primarily in architecture, but also in accepted wisdom. A process of philosophical, political, and judicial rethinking took place that was of fundamental significance, but which also led to tensions.

At the beginning of the 11th century, friction and conflicts between the archbishop and the various interest groups in Trier became more frequent and aggravated, some of which assumed grotesque elements. Sometimes they concerned the appointment to the Trier bishop's throne and sometimes the secular sovereignty of the archbishop. The city was dominated and defined essentially by privileged groups such as the noble families, members of the court, government officers; they all attempted to enrich themselves at the expense of the archbishop.

BRUNO

Their supremacy was expressed in their defensive dwelling towers, of which, among others, Franco's Tower, Jerusalem Tower at Cathedral Square, and the House of the Three Magi in Simeonstrasse, built in this tradition in the early 13th century, have been preserved.

The archbishop came into conflict not only with these groups but also with the large abbeys, especially with St. Maximin's, whose domains encompassed far more area from large bequests than those of the later Electoral State. As others before him, Archbishop Albero (1131-1152) sought to suspend the abbey's Imperial privileges, in order to place it under his sovereignty. He succeeded in his undertaking with the aid of King Conrad III (1138-1153).

A significant construction project for the city was the building of the city wall, begun under Archbishop Bruno (1102-1124). These new fortifications reduced the city's area considerably, so that only about one-third of the Roman extent remained. In the following decades, new interest groups formed who desired to influence events in the city. Their actions led to renewed tensions which lasted into the 13th century. Initially, the problem concerned the appointment to the bishop's throne.

Diese Zeit der beginnenden Gotik war eine widersprüchliche Zeit, die politisch, soziologisch und geistesgeschichtlich als uneinheitliche, differenzierte Epoche gilt. Zu den erfreulichen Ereignissen jener Zeit in Trier ist sicherlich der Neubau der Liebfrauenkirche zu rechnen, ein Juwel frühgotischer Architektur, zwischen 1235 und 1260 entstand. Die Liebfrauenkirche, der Domkreuzgang, beide unter Erzbischof Theoderich II. (1212-1242) entstanden, bildeten zusammen mit dem Dom eine einmalige Architekturgruppe, welche bis heute eine Zierde nicht nur für Trier darstellt. Im Süden vor der Stadt entstand der Neubau der Abtei St. Matthias mit einem der schönsten Dormitorien weit und breit. Aber auch der private Hausbau brachte beste Leistungen hervor, wofür das bereits erwähnte sogenannte Dreikönigenhaus in der Simeonstraße, erbaut um 1220/30, ein gutes Beispiel ist.

Das Anwachsen der Bevölkerung, das nicht zuletzt dem wirtschaftlichen Aufschwung nach dem Erstarken des Handwerks und seiner Zünfte zu verdanken war, förderte den weiteren Ausbau der Stadt. Die lockere, zum Teil noch lückenhafte Bebauung der Straßen schloß sich mehr und mehr zu einem festeren Stadtgefüge, wozu auch die Neugründung verschiedener Klöster beitrug. Es entstanden u.a. die Klöster der Franziskaner, Dominikaner, Augustiner und Karmeliter, die in einer gewissen Konkurrenz zu den altbekannten Benediktinerabteien standen.

Mit der zunehmenden Erstarkung der Handwerkerzünfte wuchs auch deren Verlangen, das städtische Leben mitbestimmen zu dürfen, da sie bisher weitgehend von aller Mitwirkung ausgeschlossen waren. Auch ihr Verlangen löste neue Streitigkeiten aus, da weder der amtierende Erzbischöfliche Schultheiß noch die herrschenden Familien oder Adelssippen ihre Macht teilen wollten. Die regulierenden Gesetze, Verordnungen und Verträge wurden meist ignoriert und waren oft nur von kurzer Dauer. Unter Erzbischof Kuno II. (1362-1388) drohte im Zusammenhang mit der über Jahrhunderte angestrebten Reichsunmittelbarkeit der Stadt gar ein Waffengang zwischen dem Erzbischof und der Stadt. Zwischen diesen Ereignissen bedrohte im Jahre 1348 der große Pestausbruch auch Trier, wodurch ein Großteil der Juden als angebliche Brunnenvergifter umgebracht wurde. Dennoch erholte sich die Stadt bald wieder und hatte nach einer Steuerliste aus dem Jahre 1364 erneut um 10 000 Einwohner. Trier konnte sich mit Städten wie Basel, Frankfurt, Hamburg oder Nürnberg messen.

Im Jahre 1377 kam es zu einer erneuten Auseinandersetzung zwischen Erzbischof und Stadtrat, die u.a. durch Zollrechte ausgelöst wurde und diesmal den Erzbischof als Verlierer sah. Dieser war über die Niederlage so verärgert, daß er noch im gleichen Jahr seine Residenz von Trier auf den Ehrenbreitstein bei Koblenz verlegte.

THEODERICH II.

The beginning Gothic period was one of contradictions, viewed as a politically, socially, and intellectually unsettled and complex era. Among the gratifying events of this period in Trier is surely the construction of the Church of Our Lady, a jewel of Early Gothic architecture, built between 1235 and 1260. With the Cathedral, Our Lady's and the Cathedral cloister, both built under Archbishop Theoderich II (1212-1242), create a unique architectural complex which is still today an adornment not only for Trier. Outside the city, in the south, the Abbey of St. Matthias was newly built, with one of the loveliest dormitories far and wide. But private house construction flourished as well, an excellent example being the above-mentioned House of the Three Magi in Simeonstrasse, built around 1220/1230.

The increase in population, owing not least to the economic upturn after the augmented power of the skilled trades and their guilds, furthered a continued development of the city. The low-density, patchy building in the city began to fill up to a more consolidated cityscape, hastend by the founding of various monastic communities within the city walls. Franciscan, Dominican, Augustinian, and Carmelite monasteries were established, providing a certain competition to the well-known Benedictine abbeys.

As the power of the guilds increased, their desire to play a role in determining events in the city also grew; before this period, they had been excluded for the most part. This very desire caused conflict, because neither the mayor appointed by the archbishop nor the ruling families or the clans of the nobility wished to share their power. The regulating laws, ordinances, and contracts were generally ignored and were often only briefly in effect. Under Archbishop Cuno II (1362-1388), even armed conflict threatened to ignite between the Archbishop and the city over its aspiration to become a free Imperial city. In 1348, amidst these events, the great outbreak of the plague also imperiled Trier, precipitating the murder of the majority of the Jewish community, who had been accused of poisoning the wells. Nevertheless, the city recovered soon and once again had about 10,000 residents, according to a tax list from 1364. Trier could match such cities as Basle, Frankfurt, Hamburg, or Nuremberg.

In 1377, renewed strife arose between Archbishop and city council over, among other things, the right to levy tolls. This time the Archbishop found himself on the losing side. He became so disgruntled that, in the ssame year, he moved his residence from Trier to the fortified castle of Ehrenbreitstein across the Rhine from Coblenz.

KUNO II

Die Zeiten beruhigten sich auch wieder, so daß der Erzbischof, er war aufgrund einer neuen Wahlordnung zur Königswahl von 1356 nunmehr auch Kurfürst des Kurstaates Trier, im Jahre 1428 gar die Hilfe der Bürgerschaft in seinem Streit mit dem reformunwilligen Domklerus erbat, die ihm auch gewährt wurde.

Nur wenig später geriet die Stadt im Zusammenhang mit der sogenannten Manderscheidschen Fehde zwischen 1430 und 1437, bei der Ulrich von Manderscheid seine Bischofswahl mit Waffengewalt durchsetzen wollte, in arge Bedrängnis. Kaum war die Stadt dieser Not entronnen, brachte die nächste Pestwelle von 1439 neues Unglück. Dennoch gingen die alten Streitigkeiten zwischen Stadt und Kurfürst weiter. Erstaunlich ist, daß im 15. Jh. trotz aller Widrigkeiten die Bautätigkeit kaum beeinflußt wurde. Am Hauptmarkt entstand die Steipe, am Kornmarkt das neue Rathaus und im Jahre 1473 eröffnete Erzbischof Johann II. (1456-1503) die neugegründete Trierer Universität. Im gleichen Jahr (1473) weilte Kaiser Friedrich III. von Habsburg (1440-1493) in Trier, um Verhandlungen mit Herzog Karl dem Kühnen von Burgund über die Vermählung von dessen Tochter, Maria von Burgund, mit seinem Sohn, Maximilian, zu führen. Als Kurfürsten wurden die Trierer Erzbischöfe natürlich gelegentlich auch in die Reichspolitik einbezogen und waren nicht selten Mitwirkende bei Entscheidungen des Kaisers. Ein ähnliches wichtiges Ereignis für die Stadt ergab sich im Jahre 1512, ein Jahr nach dem Amtsantritt des Erzbischofs Richard von Greiffenklau (1511-1531), als Kaiser Maximilian (1493-1519), noch bekannt durch seinen Besuch von 1473, einen Reichstag nach Trier einberief, der aber schon bald nach seiner Eröffnung wegen einer erneuten Pestwelle nach Köln verlegt wurde. Die von den Trierer gehegte Hoffnung, bei dieser Gelegenheit die Reichsfreiheit zu erreichen, erfüllte sich abermals nicht.

After matters calmed down once more, the Archbishop, who was now also Electoral Prince of the Electoral State of Trier by virtue of a new regulation from 1356 regarding election of the king, even requested the help of the townspeople in 1428 in his quarrel with Cathedral clergy unwilling to reform. He was granted this aid.

Only a short time later, the city came to grief when it became involved in the so-called Manderscheid Feud between 1430 and 1437, in which Ulrich of Manderscheid attempted to secure his seat on the bishop's throne by force of arms. Having barely escaped disaster, the city was faced with renewed misfortune in another outbreak of the plague in 1439. Despite this, the old conflicts between city and elector continued. It is astounding that, regardless of all the adversity, construction activity was hardly affected in the 15th century. The Steipe was built on the Main Market, the new city hall on the Grain Market and Archbishop John II (1456-1503) opened the newly founded Trier University in 1473.

In the same year (1473), Emperor Frederick III of Hapsburg (1440-1493) visited Trier to negotiate with Duke Charles the Bold of Burgundy on the marriage of Charles's daughter Mary of Burgundy, with his son Maximilian. Naturally, as electors, the Trier archbishops were also occasionally drawn into Imperial politics and were not infrequently able to influence Imperial decisions. A similarly important event for the city occurred in 1512, a year after the assumption to office by Richard of Greiffenklau (1511-1531), when Emperor Maximilian (1493-1519), still remembered from his visit of 1473, convened an Imperial Diet in Trier. It had to be removed to Cologne soon afterward, however, because of still another epidemic of the plague. Trier's cherished hopes of achieving Imperial freedom on this occasion were dashed once more.

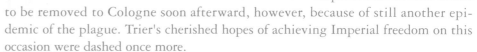

ULRICH VON MANDERSCHEID

JOHANN II. VON BADEN

RICHARD VON GREIFFENKLAU

MAXIMILIAN

Der Übergang zur Neuzeit

Nur fünf Jahre später, 1517, sollte ein anderes Ereignis tiefe Spuren in die kirchliche und politische Landschaft Deutschlands ziehen, die Reformation. In Deutschland wird dieser Zeitpunkt auch überwiegend als das Ende des Mittelalters und der Beginn der Neuzeit angesehen.

In Trier wurde der Friede allerdings wenig später von einem anderen Ereignis überschattet. Im Jahre 1522 brachte der Ritter Franz von Sickingen Furcht und Schrecken über die Stadt, als er aus Zorn über Kaiser und Erzbischof zu den Waffen griff. Er belagerte Trier mehrere Wochen erfolglos, letztlich gab er den Kampf aber auf und zog ab. Wenig später durchzogen, ausgelöst durch die Bauernkriege, erneut Unruhen das Land. Die Reformation wurde in Trier zunächst mit Zurückhaltung aufgenommen und gewann Anhänger erst um die Mitte des Jahrhunderts, nachdem sich die Bürgerschaft gespalten hatte. Ein Teil der Bürger war protestantisch gesinnt und versuchte erneut, die Reichsfreiheit zu erkämpfen, was Religionsfreiheit bedeutet hätte. Zur Auseinandersetzung kam es erst, als der Theologe Caspar Olevian (in Olewig bei Trier geboren) 1559 Anführer der Reformation wurde.

Letztlich obsiegte der Erzbischof, wer nicht zum katholischen Glauben zurückkehren wollte, mußte die Stadt verlassen. Unter den Auswanderern waren auch führende Persönlichkeiten des Geistes- und Wirtschaftslebens. 1565 brach abermals ein Streit um die Reichsunmittelbarkeit aus, in dessen Verlauf gar eine Blockade durch den Kurfürst gegen die Stadt verhängt wurde, die letztlich durch die Vermittlung des Kaisers beendet wurde. Trier erhielt zunächst eine kaiserlichen Besatzung, bis ein Urteilsspruch Kaisers Rudolf II. (1576-1612) von 1580 dem Kurfürst die Landeshoheit über die Stadt bestätigte.

Wie in den Jahrhunderten davor war der Frieden auch jetzt nur von kurzer Dauer. Kurfürst und Stadtrat, dessen Rechte stark beschränkt wurden, standen sich eher feindlich gegenüber. Dem Rat blieb kaum die Möglichkeit, das Wirtschaftsleben selbst zu gestalten. Mehrere Mißernten vergrößerten noch die Not, die ihren Höhepunkt um 1600 erreichte. Man fand bald die Schuldigen, die Hexen, die mit dem Teufel im Bund standen. Dieser Wahn kostete allein zwischen 1587 und 1593 368 unschuldigen Menschen aus den Nachbargemeinden das Leben. Es war vor allem der Trierer Jesuitenpater und Professor für Moraltheologie Friedrich Spee (1591-1635), der gegen diesen unbegreiflichen Wahnsinn ankämpfte.

FRANZ
VON SICKINGEN

CASPAR OLEVIAN

FRIEDRICH SPEE

The Transition to the Modern Era

Only five years later, in 1517, another event was to leave deep gashes in the ecclesiastical and political landscape of Germany: the Protestant Reformation. In Germany, this period is also normally viewed as the end of the Middle Ages and the beginning of the Modern Era.

However, peace in Trier was overshadowed only shortly later by another event. In 1522, the robber baron Francis of Sickingen spread fear and terror over the city when he attacked out of anger at the Emperor and the Archbishop. He besieged Trier for several weeks unsuccessfully, finally giving up the struggle and withdrawing. The city was visited by renewed troubles only a short time later in the wake of the Peasants' War. Initially, the Protestant Reformation was met with reservations but gained influence by mid-century when townspeople began to take sides. Some of them were inclined toward Protestantism and attempted again to obtain the status of a free Imperial city, which would mean the townspeople could choose the religion for the city. Conflict arose only after the theologian Caspar Olevian (born in Trier) became the initiator of the Reformation in Trier in 1559.

But ultimately the Archbishop won out: whoever did not wish to return to the Catholic faith was forced to leave. Among those leaving were also leading personalities in the intellectual and economic life of the city.

In 1565, renewed conflicts erupted over the question of political independence, in the course of which the Elector even imposed a blockage on the city, ending only with the intervention of the Emperor. In the meantime, Trier was occupied by Imperial troops until Emperor Rudolf II (1576-1612) handed down a judgment in 1580 confirming the Elector's sovereignty over the city.

As in previous centuries, peace was of short duration. Elector and city council, whose rights had been starkly curtailed, faced each other as enemies. It was hardly possible for the council to influence economic life. Several bad harvests increased the need in the city and countryside, reaching its peak around 1600. The guilty were soon found: the witches, who were in league with the devil. In just the seven years between 1587 and 1593, this hysteria cost the lives of 368 innocent people from neighboring communities. It was primarily the Trier Jesuit priest and professor of moral theology Friedrich Spee (1591-1635) who fought against this incomprehensible madness.

Auch im 17. Jh. blieb das Unheil, diesmal als Folge des Dreißigjährigen Krieges, der Stadt treu. Durch die fragwürdige Politik und den Beitritt des Kurfürsten Philipp Christoph von Sötern (1623-1652) zur sogenannten Liga, die von den Spaniern unterstützt wurde und ein Gegenbündnis zur protestantischen Union war, geriet der Kurstaat in den Strudel der Ereignisse. Trier war Durchzugsgebiet verschiedener Streitkräfte und hatte durch den Streit zwischen Franzosen und Spaniern, besonders durch die wechselnden Besatzungen und deren Versorgung, viel Leid zu ertragen. Als Philipp Christoph 1652 im Alter von 85 Jahren starb, hatte er 28 regiert, davon waren nicht weniger als 22 Kriegsjahre.

Trier wurde mehrmals von den Franzosen durchzogen und besetzt, abermals ab dem Jahr 1671. 1674 bauten sie die Stadt gar zur Festung aus. Dazu ließen sie sämtliche Vororte und die vor der Stadt liegenden Klöster, darunter St. Maximin, St. Martin, das Stift Paulin, Löwenbrücken usw. zerstören, die Stadt wurde ausgeplündert. Um diese Zeit hatte Trier noch gerade einmal 2.886 Einwohner.

An Stelle der dringend benötigten längeren Erholungsphase wütete schon bald der neu entfachte Spanische Erbfolgekrieg (1701-1714) in den deutschen Landen. Bereits 1702 wurde Trier Opfer der Auseinandersetzung zwischen Frankreich und Holland. Die Franzosen unter Ludwig dem XIV. belagerten und beschossen die Stadt und besetzten sie bis 1704. Nach kurzer Befreiung rückte die Franzosen 1705 abermals in Trier ein und blieben bis 1714. Danach erholten sich Stadt und Umland langsam, es wurde wieder gebaut. So wurde u.a. die 1689 von den Franzosen zerstörte Moselbrücke wieder hergestellt, es entstanden wieder zwei Märkte, deren es früher fünf gegeben hatte. Infolge des Polnischen Erbfolgekrieges (1733-1738) besetzten die Franzosen Trier abermals von 1734 bis 1737. Wie bereits vorher stellten sie auch diesmal erneut hohe Forderungen an die Stadt, was zu einem abermaligen Rückschlag führte. Dennoch erholte sich die Wirtschaft bald wieder, es wurde eine rege Bautätigkeit ausgelöst, in deren Rahmen neben anderen Barock-und Rokokobauanlagen auch der Südflügel des heute noch stehenden kurfürstlichen Palastes mit seiner Prachttreppe entstand.

PHILIPP CHRISTOPH VON SÖTERN

As if cursed, the city was again visited by misfortune, this time, as a result of the Thirty Years' War. By his questionable politics, Elector Phillip Christopher of Sötern (1623-1652), who had taken up with the Catholic League supported by the Spanish against the Protestant Union, plunged the Electoral State into the maelstrom of events. As various armies marched through Trier, it was alternately occupied by the warring French and Spanish troops, which the city had to provide for, occupations which brought great suffering. When Phillip Christopher died in 1652 at the age of 85, he had ruled 28 years, of which no fewer than 22 were years of warfare.

The French marched through and occupied Trier several times, starting again in 1671. In order to fortify the city in 1674, they blew up entire settlements on the periphery as well as the structures of the monastic communities outside the walls, among them St. Maximin's, St. Martin's, St. Paulin's, St. Anne's; the city was plundered. At this time, Trier had all of 2,886 inhabitants. Instead of the urgently needed long period of recovery, the recently ignited War of the Spanish Succession (1701-1714) reached the German countryside soon afterwards. As early as 1702, Trier fell victim to the strife between France and Holland. Under Louis XIV, the French besieged and cannonaded the city and occupied it until 1704. After a brief liberation, the French marched in again in 1705 and remained until 1714. City and countryside recovered slowly and rebuilding began sporadically. For example, the Moselle bridge blown up by the French in 1689 was restored; two markets of the original five were reestablished.

As a result of the War of the Polish Succession (1733-1738), the French occupied Trier once again, from 1734 to 1737. As in the past, they placed great demands on the city, creating another set-back. Nevertheless, the economy recovered soon afterward; brisk building activity began, producing, among other structures, baroque and rococo houses as well as the south wing of the still existing Electoral Palace with its magnificent staircase.

LUDWIG XIV.

Das 18. Jahrhundert war aber auch die Zeit eines neuen Denkens, das durch seine weltlichen und kirchlichen Reformen alte Denkweisen aufbrach. Unter Kurfürst Clemens Wenzeslaus von Sachsen und Polen (1768-1801), der ein Mann von aufgeklärter Bildung war, kam es zu Veränderungen im Land, deren Auswirkungen bis in unsere Zeit reichen. So war nicht zuletzt seine Anordnung, die Rieslingrebe an der Mosel anzubauen, Grundlage für die spätere Berühmtheit des Moselweines. Er ließ die Häuser der Stadt erstmals durchnumerieren und führte eine neue Brandschutzverordnung ein. Eine weitere wichtige Maßnahme war das Verbot der kleinen Pfarrfriedhöfe innerhalb des Stadtgebietes. Unter Clemens Wenzeslaus erreichte die Trierer Geschichte aber auch einen ihrer dramatischsten Höhepunkte. Im Jahre 1789 warf ein Ereignis europäischer Tragweite seine Schatten auch wieder über den Trierer Kurstaat und seine Hauptstadt, die französische Revolution, letztlich Auslöser einer Reihe von Kriegen, die Europa ein viertel Jahrhundert lang überzogen. Durch die Aufrüstung der zahlreichen französischen Emigranten im Trierer Kurstaat und den Einmarsch der Koalitionstruppen nach Frankreich kam es zu Spannungen, die 1792 zum Angriff der französischen Revolutionstruppen u.a. auch auf Trier führten, das zuvor von 1737 an von allen französischen Eroberungsversuchen verschont geblieben war. Mit der Besetzung der Stadt und des Trierer Kurstaates 1794 war auch dessen Ende gekommen. Im Oktober 1794 verließ der letzte Trierer Kurfürst, Clemens Wenzeslaus, der in Trier unbeliebt war, seine Residenz Koblenz, in die er nicht mehr zurückkehren sollte. 1801 mußte Clemens Wenzeslaus als Kurfürst abdanken und fand nach seinem Tod im Jahre 1812 seine letzte Ruhe fern von Trier in Marktoberdorf im Bistum Augsburg. Die Franzosen besetzten das gesamte linke Rheinufer. Alle Kirchengüter wurden beschlagnahmt, die Klöster und Stifte aufgehoben, sie wurden zum Teil als Kasernen, Lazarette oder Magazine genutzt. Viele Kirchen, einschließlich des Trierer Doms, wurden entweiht, ausgeraubt, als Ställe benutzt oder zerstört. Es entstand ein unwiederbringlicher Verlust an Kunst- und Kulturwerten. Die Enteignung des kirchlichen Besitzes ließ auch das eingespielte und funktionierende alte Ertragssystem der großen Weingüter und landwirtschaftlichen Höfe zusammenbrechen. In Trier, mittlerweile Hauptstadt des französischen Saardepartements mit einem Präfekten an der Spitze, stand das Wirtschaftsleben durch den rigorosen Umbruch vor dem Ruin, der die Menschen an die Grenze des Erträglichen, und manchmal auch darüber hinaus, belastete. Wie einst das römische Staatswesen und mit ihm das römische Trier ihr Ende gefunden hatten, endete die fast tausendjährige mittelalterliche Ordnung und mit ihr der Trierer Kurstaat.

CLEMENS
WENZELSLAUS

But the 18th century was also a period of new ways of thinking, brought about by secular and ecclesiastical reforms of old mindsets. Under Elector Clemens Wenzeslaus of Saxony and Poland (1768-1801), a man of the Enlightenment, transformations occurred in the state, the results of which are felt in our own time. For example, not the least of his accomplishments, the edict to plant the Riesling grape on the Moselle, formed the basis for the later fame of Moselle wine. He had houses numbered for the first time and introduced a new fire protection ordinance. A further important measure was the prohibition of the small parish cemeteries within the city walls.

Also under Clemens Wenzeslaus, however, Trier's history reached one of its dramatic high points. In 1789, a momentous event cast its shadow across Europe, reaching the Electoral State and its capital as well: the French Revolution, the ultimate trigger for a series of wars which overran Europe for a quarter of a century. Although the city had been spared all French attempts at conquest since 1737, that changed when numerous French emigrés in the Trier Electoral State armed themselves and Austrian, Prussian, and Russian troops marched into France. Tensions rose and led to attacks by French Revolutionary troops in 1792, in Trier and elsewhere. With the occupation of the city and the Trier Electoral State in 1794, this State came to an end. In October 1794, the last Trier Elector, Clemens Wenzeslaus, unpopular in Trier, left his residence in Coblenz, to where he was never to return. In 1801, he was forced to abdicate as Elector and, after his death in 1812, found his last resting place in Marktoberdorf in the Augsburg diocese, far from Trier.

The French occupied the entire area west of the Rhine. All Catholic Church property was confiscated, the monastic communities and foundations dissolved; some became barracks, field hospitals, or storehouses. Many churches, including Trier Cathedral, were profaned, plundered, used as stables, or destroyed. The entire Rhineland suffered an irreparable loss of artistic and cultural assets. The expropriation of Church property caused a collapse of the well-functioning former production system of the large wineries and agricultural estates. Because of the radical transformation, economic life in Trier, now capital of the French Saar Département with a prefect at its head, was faced with ruin which burdened the people to the utmost and sometimes even beyond. As once the Roman state and with it Roman Trier came to an end, so too did almost a thousand years of medieval order and with it the Trier Electoral State.

Abbildung Seite 13: Karte des heutigen Trier
Die ockerfarbene Markierung zeigt die mittelalterliche Stadtmauer und somit die Stadtgrenzen der mittelalterlichen Stadt um 1400 n. Chr. Die gelben Punkte (siehe Legende Seite 18) zeigen die Standorte der mittelalterlichen Bauten im heutigen Stadtbild an. Einige von ihnen sind heute überbaut bzw. nicht mehr sichtbar.

Illustration page 13: Map of modern Trier.
The yellow double line shows the former medieval city wall and thus the boundaries of the medieval city around AD 1400. The red circles (see legend on page 18) show the location of the medieval structures in the modern cityscape. Some of them have been built over or are no longer visible.

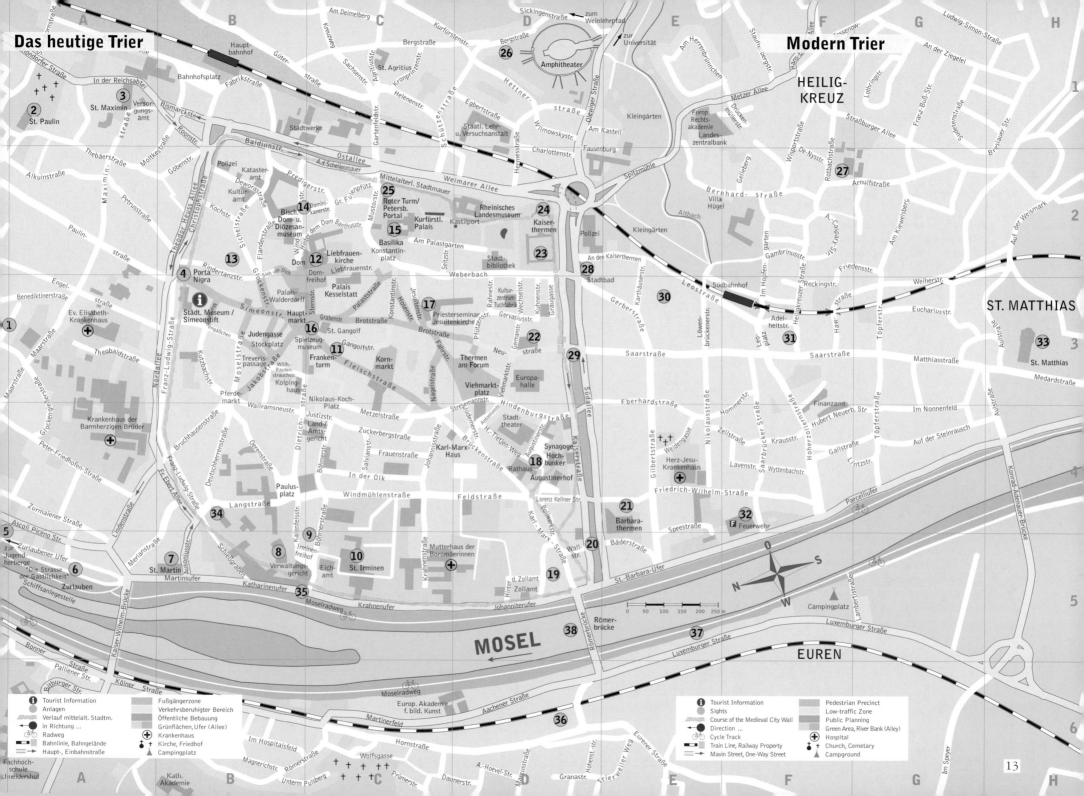

Das heutige Trier

Modern Trier

HEILIG-KREUZ

ST. MATTHIAS

MOSEL

EUREN

13

Plan des römischen Trier zu Beginn des 5. Jhs.
Map of Roman Trier at the beginning of the 5th century

Im frühen Mittelalter dürfte es in der Stadt noch keine Veränderungen gegeben haben, die den römischen Stadtplan beeinflußt hätten. Der hier vorgelegte Stadtplan des frühen 5. Jhs. dient der Orientierung und dem Vergleich mit der Situation im Mittelalter, wie auf dem Stadtplan um 1400 (Abb. 3) darstellt. Die wesentlichen Anlagen sind der folgenden Numerierung zu entnehmen:

In the Early Middle Ages, probably no alterations occurred that would have influenced the Roman layout. The city map from the early 5th century presented here serves as orientation and as a comparison to the layout in the Middle Ages, as shown on the map from around 1400 (illustration 3). The most important places and structures have the following numbers on the map:

1	Nördliches Gräberfeld (Nordfriedhof)
1A	Coemeterialbau im Bereich von St. Maximin, St. Paulin liegt außerhalb des Planausschnittes
2	Nördliches Stadttor (Porta Nigra)
3	Triumphbogen in der Simeonstraße
4	Kirchenanlage mit Dom
5	Palastaula (Basilika)
6	Zirkusanlage
7	Amphitheater
8	Tempel am Herrenbrünnchen
9	Kaiserthermen (Kaiserpalast)
10	Tempelbezirk im Altbachtal
11	Forum
12	Vermuteter Victorinuspalast
13	Großer Wohnpalast
13a	Hochschule? Sportanlage?
14	Horrea
15	Asclepius-Tempel
16	Ehrenbogen am Bollwerk
17	Barbarathermen
18	Töpferbezirk
19	Südliches Stadttor („Porta Media")
20	Südliches Gräberfeld, St. Eucharius (später St. Matthias) liegt außerhalb des Planausschnittes
21	Ältere Moselbrücke (Pfahlrostbrücke)
22	Moselbrücke (heutige Römerbrücke)
23	Rundbau (Exedra) zur Pfahlrostbrückenanlage gehörend
24	Tempelbezirk mit Lenus-Mars-Tempel
25	Viehmarktthermen
26	Ruwerwasserleitung
27	Südöstliches Stadttor („Porta Alba")

1.	North cemetery
1A.	Cemetery building in the area of St. Maximin's. St. Paulin's is located outside the confines of the map
2.	North city gate (Porta Nigra)
3.	Triumphal arch in Simeonstrasse
4.	Church complex with Cathedral
5.	Imperial throne room ("Basilika")
6.	Circus
7.	Amphitheater
8.	Temple at Herrenbrünnchen
9.	Imperial Baths (Imperial Palace)
10.	Temple district in the Altbach Valley
11.	Forum
12.	Postulated palace of Victorinus
13.	large dwelling palace
13a.	Academy? sports facility?
14.	Roman storehouses (*horrea*)
15.	Aesculapius temple
16.	Triumphal arch at Am Bollwerk
17.	Barbara Baths
18.	Potters' district
19.	South city gate ("Porta Media")
20.	South cemetery; St. Eucharius's (later St. Matthias's) is located outside the confines of the map
21.	Older Moselle bridge (wooden pier bridge)
22.	Moselle bridge (present-day Roman Bridge)
23.	Circular structure (*exedra*) belonging to wooden pier bridge
24.	Temple district with Lenus-Mars Temple
25.	Forum Baths
26.	Ruwer water conduit
27.	Southeast city gate ("Porta Alba")

Stadtansicht des römischen Trier zu Beginn des 5. Jhs.
View of Trier at the beginning of the 5th century

Diese Rekonstruktion zeigt die noch geschlossene Stadtbebauung mit ihrem typischen quadratischen Straßennetz, ein unverkennbares Kennzeichen der römischen Stadt, aus dem sich die weitflächigen Großbauten gut sichtbar herausheben. Ob die großen Bäderanlagen zu dieser Zeit noch in Betrieb waren, ist fraglich, mit Sicherheit haben die Germaneneinfälle Einschränkungen, Störungen oder gar Zerstörungen mit sich gebracht. Durch den Bericht eines Zeitzeugen wissen wir, daß die Bevölkerung, trotz der schweren Zeit und trotz des starken Rückgangs durch die Verlegung von Kaiserhof und Präfektur, immer noch Zirkusspiele forderte. Die Verringerung der Einwohnerzahl dürfte sich auf das Stadtgefüge zu dieser Zeit noch nicht wesentlich ausgewirkt haben. Bei diesem Bild wurde im Norden, Süden und Westen der Stadt zugunsten der größeren Darstellung der Innenstadt auf die Wiedergabe der nördlich von St. Maximin (Nordfriedhof) liegenden Paulinkirche, einen Teil der südlichen Stadtmauer und den weiter außerhalb liegenden Südfriedhof sowie den Tempelbezirk des Lenus-Mars im Westen verzichtet. Siehe dazu auch Stadtplan Abb. 1.

This reconstruction shows the still compact cityscape with its typical pattern of square city blocks, an unmistakable mark of a Roman city, from which the large structures stand out visibly. Whether the great bathing facilities were still in operation at this time is questionable; most certainly, the Germanic invasions brought about constrictions, disturbances, or even destruction. From the report of a contemporary witness, we know that the inhabitants, despite the difficult times and with their numbers diminished by the transfer of the Imperial court and the prefecture, continued to demand chariot races in the Circus. The reduction of the population probably did not essentially affect the city's structure at that time.
In order to represent a larger section of the inner city, the picture has left out St. Paulin's north of St. Maximin's (north cemetery), a section of the city wall on the south side, the south cemetery further outside the wall, and the temple district of Lenus-Mars on the west side of the city (see map, illustration 1).

Blick auf das heutige Trier von Westen / Trier today seen from the West:

Porta Nigra	Dom / Liebfrauen	Basilika	Petrisberg	Kaiserthermen	Römerbrücke
Porta Nigra	Cathedral / Our Lady	Basilika	Petrisberg Mountain	Imperial Baths	Roman Bridge

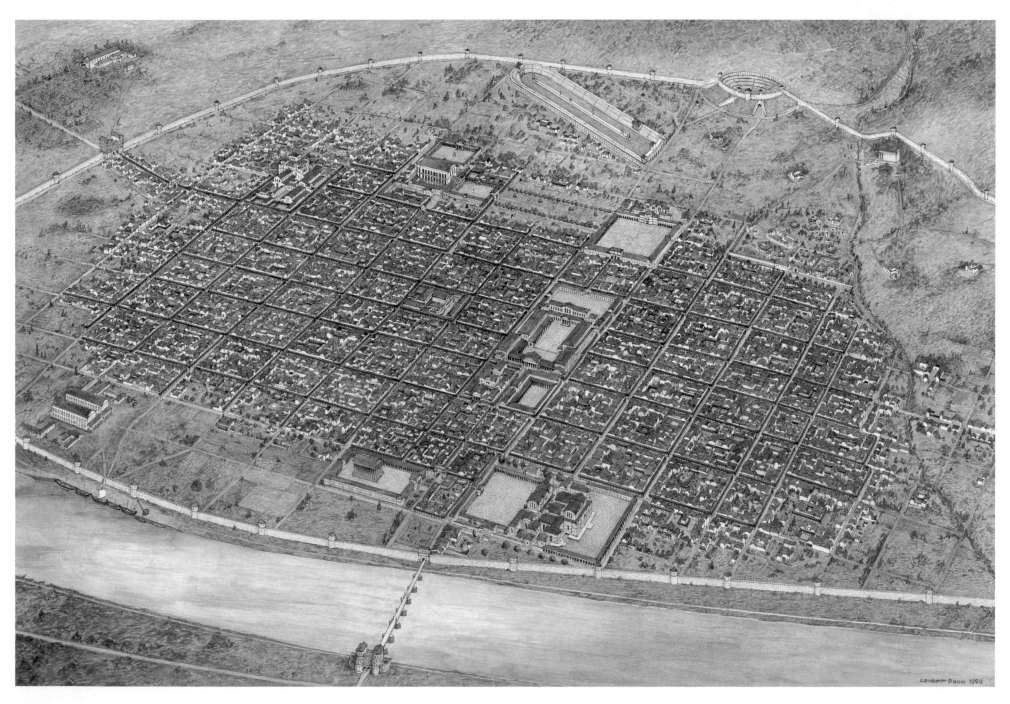

Plan des mittelalterlichen Trier um 1400
Map of Medieval Trier around 1400

Die Verkleinerung der Stadtfläche gegenüber dem Plan der Stadt des 5. Jh. (Abb. 1) ist offensichtlich. Die klare Ordnung des römischen Straßennetzes besteht nicht mehr, die Klöster und Kirchen sind nunmehr die wichtigen Bauanlagen, deren Lage wie folgt numeriert ist:

In contrast to the map of the city in the 5th century (illustration 1), this map demonstrates the manifest reduction in the city's area. The defined order of the Roman network of streets no longer exists; the monastic communities and churches are now the important structures, numbered as follows:

1	Kloster St. Marien (ad Martyres),	1. St. Mary's (ad Martyres) monastery
2	Stift und Kirche St. Paulin,	2. St. Paulin's Collegiate Foundation and Church
3	Kloster St. Maximin,	3. Abbey of St. Maximin
4	Porta Nigra mit Kirche und Stift St. Simeon sowie das Simeontor,	4. Porta Nigra with St. Simeon's Collegiate Foundation and Church
5	St. Remigius,	5. St. Remigius's
6	Kloster St. Symphorian,	6. St. Symphorian's monastery
7	Kloster St. Martin,	7. St. Martin's Abbey
8	Kloster St. Katharinen,	8. Convent of St. Katharine
9	Kirche St. Paulus,	9. Church of St. Paul
10	Kloster St. Irminen (Oeren),	10. Convent of St. Irmina (Oeren)
11	Karmeliterkloster,	11. Carmelite Convent
12	Dom und Liebfrauen (Domfreiheit punktiert),	12. Cathedral and Church of Our Lady (dotted line shows Cathedral city)
13	Haus Fetzenreich,	13. Fetzenreich house
14	Dominikanerkloster,	14. Dominican monastery
15	Palatium (Basilika) mit St. Laurentius,	15. Palatium ("Basilika") with St. Lawrence's
16	Hauptmarkt mit St. Gangolf,	16. Main Market with St. Gangolf's
17	Franziskaner-Minoriten-Kloster (Jesuiten),	17. Franciscan Friars Minor monastery (later Jesuits)
18	Augustinerkloster,	18. Augustinian monastery
19	Templerorden,	19. Knights Templar
20	St. Maria zur Brücke,	20. St. Mary's at the Bridge
21	St. Salvator (in den Barbarathermen),	21. St. Salvator's (in the Barbara Baths)
22	St. German,	22. St. Germanus's
23	St. Gervasius und St. Agneten,	23. St. Gervasius's and St. Agnes's
24	Ruine der Kaiserthermen mit Altpforte,	24. Ruin of the Imperial Baths with the Altpforte (city gate)
25	Musilpforte,	25. Musil Gate
26	römische Stadtmauer,	26. Roman city wall
27	Heiligkreuzkapelle,	27. Holy Cross Chapel
28	Weberpforte,	28. Weavers' Gate
29	Neupforte,	29. New Gate
30	Karthäuserkloster,	30. Carthusian monastery
31	Kloster St. Anna,	31. Convent of St. Anne
32	St. Barbara,	32. St. Barbara's
33	Kloster St. Matthias (St. Eucharius) mit Hoheitsbereich,	33. Abbey of St. Matthias (St. Eucharius) with monastic domains
34	Martinspforte,	34. Martin's Gate
35	Oerenpforte,	35. Oeren Gate
36	St. Isidor,	36. St. Isidor's
37	St. Viktor,	37. St. Victor's
38	Moselbrücke.	38. Moselle bridge

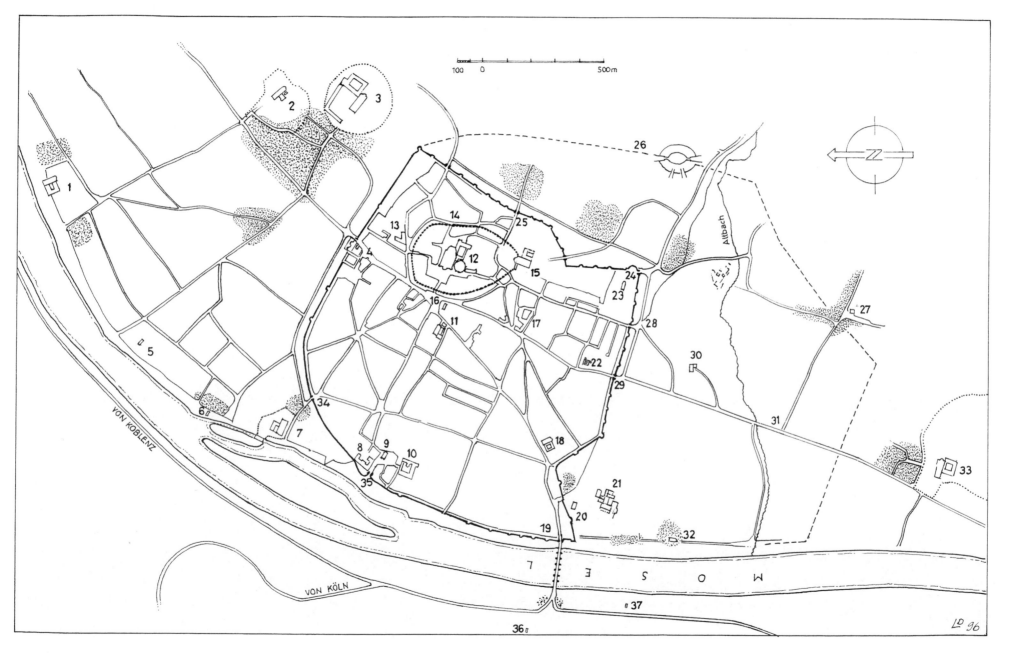

Stadtansicht von Trier in der 2. Hälfte des 14. Jhs.
View of Trier in the 2ⁿᵈ half of the 14ᵗʰ century

Dieser Rekonstruktionsversuch zeigt das Stadtbild von Trier, wie es um 1400, also 1000 Jahre später als auf der Ansicht des frühen 5. Jhs. (Abb. 2) dargestellt, ausgesehen haben könnte. Auffällig ist die sparsame Bebauung, welche sich im wesentlichen auf die Säumung der Straßen beschränkte. Neben den beiden Stifts- und Klosteranlagen von St. Paulin und St. Maximin sind die Porta Nigra als Simeonkirche, das Simeonstift, der Dom und Liebfrauen gut zu erkennen. Weiter rechts sieht man das Palatium, die heutige Basilika, mit der davorstehenden Laurentiuskirche. Deutlich zu erkennen ist auch die Dreieckform des Hauptmarktes mit der Gangolfkirche. Etwas darunter der Frankenturm und das Karmeliterkloster. Nahe der Mosel lagen die Klöster St. Martin, St. Katharinen und St. Irminen sowie die alte Pauluskirche. Der Ring der Stadtmauer bezieht die Reste der Kaiserthermen mit ein. Im Bereich der Thermenpalaestra steht die alte Gervasiuskirche, daneben das Agnetenkloster. Die Barbarathermen liegen außerhalb der Stadtmauer. Die Moselbrücke ist bereits mit einer massiven gewölbten Fahrbahnkonstruktion und mit Brückentoren ausgebaut. Die weiter südlich (rechter Bildrand) liegende Abtei St. Matthias ist durch ihren großen Abstand zur Stadt nicht mehr erfaßt

This reconstruction attempt shows the layout of Trier as it might have appeared around 1400, that is, 1000 years later than the view of the city in the early 5ᵗʰ century (illustration 2). The sparseness of built-up areas is striking; houses are essentially limited to either side of the streets. Besides the collegiate and monastery buildings of St. Paulin's and St. Maximin's, the Porta Nigra as Simeon's Church, Simeon's College, the Cathedral and Church of Our Lady are all easy to recognize. The *palatium* is further to the right (the present-day "Basilika") with the Church of St. Lawrence in front of it. Also quite clearly recognizable is the triangular form of the Main Market with the Church of St. Gangolf. Slightly below that are Franco's Tower and the Carmelite Convent. St. Martin's Abbey, the Convents of St. Katharine and of St. Irmina, and the old Church of St. Paul are located near the Moselle. The ring forming the city wall incorporates the remains of the Imperial Baths. The old Gervasius Church, with the neighboring Convent of St. Agnes, stands on the sports grounds of the old bath. The Barbara Baths are outside the city wall. The Moselle bridge has already received a massive vaulted roadway structure and bridge gates. The Abbey of St. Matthias located further south (right side of picture) is not visible because of its distance from the city.

Blick auf das heutige Trier von Osten
Trier today seen from the east

Lambert Dahm 96'

Die Kirchenanlage mit dem Dom als Zentrum zu Beginn des 5. Jhs.
The Church complex with the Cathedral as the center, beginning of the 5th century

Zu dieser Zeit war Trier bereits um die 150 Jahre Bischofssitz. Die Bischofskirche war Zentrum der hier gezeigten Kirchenanlage, die nicht weniger als vier Kirchen umfaßte. Die Rekonstruktion versucht, den komplizierten Befund dieser Anlage aus dem 4. Jh. im Bereich des heutigen Doms und der Liebfrauenkirche wiederzugeben.

Trotz aller Wirren und Kriege konnte der Dom seine Kontinuität als Bauwerk und Bischofskirche bis in unsere Zeit erhalten. Münzfunde deuten darauf hin, daß um 315, wohl unter Bischof Agritius, mit dem Bau der ersten der vier Teilkirchen, der Südwestkirche (hier vorn links) begonnen wurde, welcher schon bald die Südostkirche im Bereich der heutigen Liebfrauenkirche (nach rechts anschließend) folgte. In ihr vermutet man die eigentliche Volkskirche. Danach entstanden die Nordwest- und Nordostkirche, die Bischofskirche. Zwischen der Südost- und der Nordostkirche hatte man die Taufkapelle errichtet. Dieser im Norden einmalige Baukomplex konnte sich durchaus mit den frühchristlichen Anlagen in Rom, wie etwa der Lateranbasilika und St. Peter, welche zum Teil zeitgleich entstanden waren, messen.

Das Bild zeigt eindrucksvoll, wie sich der Quadratbau der Bischofskirche aus valentinianisch-gratianischer Zeit über das Umfeld erhebt. Er ist auch heute noch der Mittelpunkt des Doms und Standort des Hochaltars.

At this time, Trier had already been a bishop's see for about 150 years. The bishop's church was the center of the complex in this picture, comprising no fewer than four church sections. The reconstruction attempts to reflect the complicated finds from this 4th century aggregation where the present-day Cathedral and Church of Our Lady now stand. Despite all the unrest and wars, the Cathedral has been able to preserve its continuity as a structure and as the bishop's church into our own time. Coins found suggest that probably Bishop Agritius, around 315, began the construction of the first of the four church sections, the southwest church (foreground left). The southeast church, where the Church of Our Lady now stands, was constructed soon afterward (adjoining further right); it is assumed to have been the people's church. Next, the northwest and the northeast sections were built, the bishop's church. A separate baptistery was erected between the southeast and the northeast church. This complex, unique in the North of the Empire, equaled the Early Christian churches in Rome such as the Basilica of St. John Lateran and St. Peter's, both of which were erected partly during the same period.

The picture shows the spectacular square rear section of the bishop's church from the time of Emperors Valentinian and Gratian as it rises from its surroundings. Today this section remains the center of the Cathedral with the altar at its heart.

Luftaufnahme der gesamten Kirchenanlage mit Domfreihof
Aerial photo of the Cathedral complex with Cathedral Square

Lambert Dahm

Die römische Bischofskirche zu Beginn des 5. Jhs.
The Roman bishop's church at the beginning of the 5th century

Der Blick von Nordosten auf die Bischofskirche des 4. Jhs., etwa aus der Sicht der heutigen Windstraße. Dieser valentinianisch-gratianische Bau hatte bis zu seiner endgültigen Fertigstellung mehrere Jahrzehnte verschiedener Baustadien und der Bauunterbrechung erlebt, was u.a. durch die politischen Verhältnisse bedingt war. Der heute noch als Bestandteil des Doms bis z.T. auf 25 m Höhe erhaltene Quadratbau war zentraler Teil der gesamten Kirchenanlage. Der erhöhte, turmartige Mittelteil und die vier Ecktürme des Quadratbaues waren mit höchster Wahrscheinlichkeit in unveränderter Form auch Zentrum des von Bischof Nicetius im 6. Jh. wieder hergestellten Doms. Die starke Vertikalwirkung der Architektur hat man durch kräftige

Horizontalgesimse gemildert. Diese bestanden aus einer Holz-Stuck-Konstruktion, deren Balkenlöcher heute noch (ähnlich wie bei der sogen. Basilika, wo sie auch als Stützbalken einer Galerie interpretiert wurden) unter den Fenstern im antiken Mauerwerk zu erkennen sind. Die Farbigkeit des Bauwerks ist hier verhalten und nur auf einige Farbbänder beschränkt, sie könnte eher aufwendiger gewesen sein. Leider sind uns keine antiken Fassaden mit Außenmalereien erhalten, die Vorbild für eine sichere Farbrekonstruktion hätten sein können.

Blick von der Windstraße auf die römische Nordwand (Rotsandstein) des Domes
View from Windstrasse onto the Roman north wall (red sandstone) of the Cathedral

The picture shows the bishop's church of the 4th century from the northeast, more or less from present-day Windstrasse. Before it was finished, this structure from the time of the Emperors Valentinian and Gratian experienced several decades of different construction phases as well interruptions as a result of political conditions, among other reasons. Still today a part of the Cathedral, in some places 83 ft/25 m high, the square section was the center of the entire church complex. The raised, tower-like middle section and the four corner towers of this square section were most likely also the unaltered center of the Cathedral restored by Bishop Nicetius in the 6th century. The starkly vertical effect of the architecture was moderated by the thick horizontal ledges consisting of wood and plaster whose holes for the supporting beams are still visible under the windows in the ancient masonry (similar to the "Basilika," where the holes for the supporting beams suggest an outside gallery). The colors of the structure are kept muted and are limited only to a few colored bands; they could have been more elaborate, however. Unfortunately, no ancient façades have been preserved with their exterior painting which could have served as a model for a reliable color reconstruction.

Lambert Dahm 95

Der valentinianisch-gratianische Dom in der Innenansicht um 400
Interior view of the Cathedral from the period of Valentinian and Gratian, around 400

Die Rekonstruktion auf Abb. 6 zeigt das Äußere des Quadratbaus; hier soll nun dem Betrachter ein Eindruck vom Innern der Bauanlage vermittelt werden. Was Umfang und Qualität der Ausstattung betrifft, war sie wohl der Bischofskirche der Kaiserresidenz angemessen. Bei den Untersuchungen durch J. N. von Wilmowsky 1874 konnten Befunde gesichert werden, die auf marmorinkrustierte Wände und Marmorfußböden hinweisen. Darüber hinaus wurden Spuren und Reste von Mosaikschmuck an den Wänden festgestellt, die auf eine sehr gute Ausstattung schließen lassen.

Der Wandschmuck zeigte im unteren Teil, bis zu den Fensterbänken, eine farbig gemusterte Marmorinkrustation. Darüber schloß sich zwischen den Fenstern, wohl bis zu den oberen Fenstern reichend, Mosaikschmuck mit wahrscheinlich floraler Zier an. In der anschließenden Zone folgte dann bis zur Decke hin wohl eine aufgemalte Gliederung, welche wahrscheinlich an die Marmorverkleidung der unteren Wandzone orientiert war, nur weit leichter in der Farbgebung. Der Altar, in der hier dargestellten Form nicht belegt, stand wie auch die vier den turmartigen Mittelbau stützenden Granitsäulen auf einem Podium, dessen fünf Stufen ergraben wurden. Ein Fragment einer der vier Granitsäulen liegt heute vor dem Südwestportal des Doms.

Innenansicht des Domes mit Blick nach Osten
Interior of the Cathedral looking east

Illustration 6 reconstructs the exterior of the square section of the Cathedral; illustration 7 gives the viewer an impression of the interior of the church. Size and quality of the furnishings were surely consistent with the bishop's church of an Imperial residence. The finds by J. N. von Wilmowsky in 1874 suggest marble-covered walls and marble floors. Moreover, traces and remains of mosaic decoration on the walls were identified that suggest lavish appointments.

In the lower level, up to the window sills, the wall decoration displayed a colorful pattern of marble inlay. Above that, probably reaching to the upper windows, mosaics decorated the walls in between the windows, presumably with floral patterns. On the final section of wall up to the ceiling, the decoration was likely painted, probably oriented on the marble work in the lower sections, only lighter in color.

Although not documented as pictured, the altar stood, as did the four granite columns supporting the tower-like middle section, on a dais whose five steps have been excavated. Today, a section of one of the four columns lies to the left of the southwest Cathedral portal.

Der Domstein - ein Fragment einer der Granitsäulen
Cathedral Stone - a section of one of the Roman granite columns

Innenansicht der Domkirche nach 600
Interior of the Cathedral after 600

Der valentinianisch-gratianische Dom lag nach den Germaneneinfällen wahrscheinlich längere Zeit in unbrauchbarem oder stark eingeschränktem Benutzungszustand, ehe er im 6. Jh. auf Veranlassung von Bischof Nicetius, wohl in der alten Form des späten 4. Jhs., wieder hergestellt wurde. Die Außenmauern des Quadratbaues waren kaum zerstört, wohl aber die Säulen und die Bögen in der Vierung. Sie wurden durch Kalksteinsäulen aus dem 2. Jh. ersetzt, welche vom römischen Tempel am Herrenbrünnchen stammen sollen. Die Fenster wurden durch Aufmauerung der Bänke um etwa 0,55 m kleiner. Mit dem Zerstörungsschutt hatte man den Boden im gesamten Quadratbau um etwa vier Treppenstufen erhöht, wodurch das westlich anschließende Langhaus um etwa 0,90 m, eben die genannten vier Treppenstufen, tiefer lag.
Die Rekonstruktion gibt einen Zustand um 600

Ummauerte römische Kalksteinsäule mit Maskenkapitell
Walled-over Roman column with figure capital

Kreuzpfeiler stabilisieren heute die Kalksteinsäulen
Cross-shaped piers stabilize the limestone columns today

wieder, nachdem bereits, wohl in nachnicetischer Zeit, ein hufeisenförmiger Ambo eingebaut war, ein Vorgänger der späteren Kanzel. Außer dem Ambo konnte J. N. von Wilmowsky bei seiner Grabung 1874 auch die Reste eines Ziegelbodens beobachten, mit dem das Kirchenschiff ausgelegt war. Die Holzdecke war mit größter Wahrscheinlichkeit offen, wie dies auch in den späteren Jahrhunderten noch üblich war. Gegenüber der Anlage des 4. Jhs. (Abb. 7) wirkt dieser Kirchenbau weniger repräsentativ und festlich, die Einfachheit der Romanik kündigt sich bereits an.

After the Germanic invasions, the Roman Cathedral no doubt stood in such a state as to be unusable or its use greatly reduced, before it was restored in the 6th century by Bishop Nicetius to its old form of the late 4th century. The outer walls of the square section were more or less preserved, but not the columns and arches in the crossing. They were replaced by limestone columns from the 2nd century, said to have come from the Roman temple at Herrenbrünnchen. The raised windowsills reduced the height of the windows by 22 in/55 cm. With the rubble, the floor level in the entire square section was raised by about four steps, thus leaving the adjoining nave and side aisles 3 ft/90 cm lower, just the height of the mentioned four steps.
The reconstruction in the picture renders a state around 600 after a horseshoe-shaped ambo, a precursor to the later pulpit, had been built in the church, probably following Nicetius' time. During his excavations in 1874, Wilmowsky observed, besides the ambo, the remains of a tile floor in the church nave. In all likelihood, the wooden ceiling was open, as was customary in later centuries. In contrast to the church of the 4th century (illustration 7), this church structure appears less imposing and majestic; the simplicity of Romanesque is already foreshadowed here.

Lambert Dahm 1994

Seitenansicht des Doms von Nordosten um 1100
Side view of the Cathedral from the northeast, around 1100

Der Dom ist hier etwa der Abb. 6 gleich, nur aus größerer Höhe gesehen. Sein Ostteil zeigt noch die kaum veränderte Architektur des römischen Domes aus dem 4. beziehungsweise 6. Jahrhundert. Der popponische Westteil mit den Türmen und der Westapsis ist bereits einige Zeit vollendet.

Leider gibt es keinerlei Anhalt für das Aussehen des Quadratbaues, die Rekonstruktion geht daher von Wahrscheinlichkeiten aus. Mit Ausnahme der Fenster und dem Fehlen der ausgeprägten Gesimse dürfte der Bau kaum verändert worden sein. Er ist schmuckloser, eben durch das Fehlen der Horizontalgesimse, welche die starke Vertikalwirkung der Architektur weitgehend gemildert hatten. Eine ähnliche Wirkung könnte allerdings durch Farbbänder innerhalb einer Farbfassung erreicht worden sein, die man sich als Teil der Gesamtkonzeption vorzustellen hat. Es zeigt sich hier eine sehr ausgewogene Architektur, einmal durch den turmartigen Mittelteil des Quadratbaues und die vier seitlichen Türme, zum anderen durch die popponische Westfront mit den beiden großen Türmen und den zwei seitlichen runden Treppentürmen als Gegengewicht. Man könnte sich vorstellen, daß die Osttürme Vorbild für die Architektur der Westtürme waren, wodurch die architektonische Einheit der Kirche erreicht wurde. In der zweiten Hälfte des 12 Jhs. veränderte sich der Blick durch die unter Erzbischof Hillin (1152-1169) angebaute romanische Ostapsis.

Ansicht des Domes von Nordosten
View of the Cathedral from the northeast

The Cathedral in this picture is about the same as in illustration 6 but seen from a greater height. Its east section still displays the hardly altered architecture of the Roman Cathedral from the 4th century or the 6th century. The west section built under Archbishop Poppo with the towers and the west apse had been finished for some time.

Unfortunately, there are no clues to the appearance of the square section; the reconstruction is thus based on probabilities. With the exception of the windows and the ledges, the building has hardly changed. It is less decorated because of the lack of horizontal ledges which had moderated the strong vertical effect of the architecture. A similar effect, however, could have been created by colored bands as a part of a painted façade included in an overall design.

A well-balanced architecture is presented here, first because of the tower-like middle section of the square and the four side towers, and, second, because of the west section with the two great towers and the two flanking round stair towers as a counterbalance. We can imagine that the east towers served as models for the architecture of the west towers, creating an architecturally unified church structure. In the second half of the 12th century, the appearance of the church was altered by the Romanesque east apse added under Archbishop Hillin (1152-1169).

Lambert Dahm 95

Der Dom um 1250, von Nordwesten gesehen
The Cathedral around 1250, seen from the northwest

Der Dom hat im wesentlichen sein heutiges Aussehen, abgesehen von dem später erhöhten Südwestturm. Ungewohnt für uns heute sind der Verputz und die Farbigkeit, die mit größter Wahrscheinlichkeit so oder ähnlich gegeben waren. Auf den ältesten Fotoaufnahmen und älteren Zeichnungen, zum Beispiel von J. A. Ramboux aus dem Jahre 1828, sind noch große Putzflächen, auch an den beiden Türmen, zu erkennen. J. N. von Wilmowsky hatte zudem in den Galerieräumen in den Türmen Reste des alten, sehr hellen Verputzes festgestellt. Das völlige Entfernen des Verputzes war wohl ein Zugeständnis an den Zeitgeist der Romantik im 19. Jh., der eine Vorliebe für ruinenhaft anmutendes Mauerwerk hatte. Diese Zeit stand der Farbe am Bau und an der Plastik fast feindlich gegenüber, alte Farbfassungen wurden häufig rücksichtslos entfernt. Die dadurch entstandenen Verluste sind unersetzbar.

Das Bild zeigt, daß um die Mitte des 13. Jhs. die Liebfrauenkirche gerade im Bau war, sie wurde um 1260 vollendet. Zu den fehlenden Außengerüsten ist zu sagen, daß die Baugerüste bei nicht verputzten Bauwerken oft nur innen hochgezogen wurden. Die unterschiedlichen Baukräne zum Hochziehen der Steine und anderer Baumaterialien wurden mit dem Wachsen des Mauerwerks und des Gerüstes höhergesetzt. Diese bautechnischen Vorgänge sind auf Zeichnungen jener Zeit belegt.

The Cathedral has essentially its present appearance, except for the southwest tower raised later. Unusual for us today are the stuccoed walls and color, which were probably as pictured, or at least similar. In the oldest photos and older drawings, for example, those by Johann Anton Ramboux from 1828, large patches of stucco are visible, even on both towers. J. N. von Wilmowsky found, moreover, remains of the old, very light-colored plaster in the galleries in the towers. The complete removal of the stucco was doubtless a concession to the spirit of the Romantic age in the 19th century, which had a preference for ruin-like masonry. It was an age almost hostile to color on buildings and sculpture; old paint or colored stucco was frequently ruthlessly eradicated. Such loses are irreparable.

The picture shows that the Church of Our Lady was being built around the mid-13th century; it was finished around 1260. As to the absence of exterior scaffolding, it must be said that scaffolding was often put up only in the interior of an unstuccoed building. The different construction cranes to hoist the stones and other building materials were set higher as the walls and scaffolding grew higher. Such technical procedures are documented in drawings of the time.

Blick auf den heute unverputzten Dom und auf Liebfrauen
View of the unstuccoed Cathedral and Church of Our Lady

Kurie Metzenhausen neben dem Dom
Metzenhausen clergy house next to the Cathedral

Das Domviertel war seit dem frühen Mittelalter auch bevorzugter Wohnbereich der Domkleriker. Ihre Kurien standen in den zum Teil noch heute erhaltenen Gassen um den Dom, die um 1000 durch die sogenannte Ludolfsche Mauer von der übrigen Stadt getrennt wurden. Von den frühen Kurien ist nichts erhalten, erst aus gotischer Zeit sind geringe Baureste auf uns gekommen. Teilweise wurden sie durch Barockbauten ersetzt, welche den Verlust wohl zum Teil verschmerzen lassen.

Das Bild zeigt die Kurie Metzenhausen, wie sie um 1600 ausgesehen haben könnte. Der Bau wurde an Stelle der älteren und verfallenen Kurie Hünerberg im Jahre 1530 errichtet und gilt als erster profaner Bau der Renaissance in Trier. Die bildliche Überlieferung verdanken wir einer Bleistiftzeichnung von Joh. Anton Ramboux aus

dem Jahre 1828, die zwei Jahre vor dem Abbruch entstand. Die Kurie stand gegenüber dem ehemaligen Dominikanerkloster des 13. Jhs., das nach der Säkularisation zum Gefängnis umfunktioniert wurde. Die Kurie, im Jahre 1794 von den Franzosen beschlagnahmt, ging 1830 in den Besitz der Stadt über, die sie abbrach und in den Jahren 1832/33 durch einen Gefängnisneubau ersetzte.

Diese Rekonstruktion versucht, auf der Grundlage von Ramboux, den Zustand der vorbarocken Zeit um 1600 wiederzugeben. Der gewählte Blick, mit der Domgruppe im Hintergrund, zeigt die Kirche noch vor ihrer barocken Umgestaltung, die erst nach dem Brand von 1717 erfolgte.

Das Bischöfliche Dom- und Diözesanmuseum auf dem Gelände der Kurie Metzenhausen (Pfeil)
The Bishop's Museum on the grounds of the Metzenhausen clergy house (arrow)

Since the Early Middle Ages, the Cathedral clergy had also preferred to live in the Cathedral city. Their clergy houses are located in the still preserved lanes around the Cathedral, which was segregated from the rest of the city around 1000 by a wall built under Archbishop Ludolf. Nothing exists today of the early clergy houses; only a few remains from the Gothic era are preserved. Some were replaced by baroque houses which make up in part for the losses.

The picture shows the Metzenhausen clergy house as it might have looked around 1600. In 1530, it was built where the older and dilapidated Hünerberg house stood and is considered to have been the first secular Renaissance structure in Trier. A pictorial document exists thanks to a pencil drawing by J. A. Ramboux in 1828, made two years before the house was demolished. The house stood opposite the former Dominican monastery from the 13th century, which was converted into the prison following the secularization of the French Revolutionary era. Confiscated by the French in 1794, the house reverted to the city in 1830; it was torn down and replaced by a new prison building in 1832/33. The reconstruction attempt, based on Ramboux, reflects the appearance during the pre-baroque era around 1600. The viewpoint chosen, with the Cathedral in the background, shows the church before the baroque remodeling, which took place following a fire in 1717.

Lambert Dahm 99

Das Coemeterialgebäude auf dem Nordfriedhof Anfang des 5. Jhs.
The cemetery building in the north cemetery at the beginning of the 5th century

Dieser Rekonstruktionsversuch zeigt den Nordfriedhof mit einer Bauanlage, die dem Bestattungsbrauchtum diente. Die gesamte Entwicklung des Friedhofs und der Bauanlage ist im engen Zusammenhang mit der wachsenden Verehrung der dort im 4. Jh. bestatteten Trierer Bischöfe Agritius und Maximin, besonders letzterem, zu sehen. Das hier gezeigte Hauptgebäude ist in der zweiten Hälfte des 4. Jhs. entstanden. Es war ein fast 100 m langer und 17 m breiter Bau, der durch Anbauten und Inkorporation älterer Bauteile, darunter auch die Grabgrüfte der hl. Bischöfe, basilikaähnlich wirkte. Die Bischöfe galten nach ihrer Heiligsprechung als Fürsprecher der Trierer Bevölkerung. Es ist davon ausgehen, daß ihre Gräber in den Unruhezeiten des 5. Jhs. nicht ohne Schutz waren und wahrscheinlich von frommen Männern bewacht wurden. Sie könnten in einer Gemeinschaft gelebt haben, welche als Grundstock des Klosters gesehen werden darf.

Dem großen Coemeterialgebäude gingen mehrere Bauperioden verschieden großer Grabhäuser und Bestattungsanlagen voraus, von denen noch kleinere Bauteile im Mauerwerk des neuen Coemeterialgebäudes erhalten waren. Die an der Nordseite der Bestattungshalle angebauten Grabkammern waren wahrscheinlich Begräbnisstätten privilegierter Familien oder Sippen. Der Gesamtumfang des Friedhofs konnte durch spätere Überbauung bisher noch nicht erfaßt werden.

Luftaufnahme auf St. Maximin mit Blick von Südosten
Aerial photo of St. Maximin's with a view from the southeast

This reconstruction attempt shows the north cemetery with a structure which served existing burial customs. The entire development of the cemetery and the structure may be viewed in close association with the growing veneration of the Trier Bishops Agritius and Maximinus, buried there in the 4th century, especially of the latter. The main structure, shown here, was erected in the second half of the 4th century, almost 330 ft/100 m long and 56 ft/17 m wide. It gained the appearance of a basilica through extensions and incorporations of older sections, among them also the mausoleums of the bishops. These bishops, venerated as saints, were considered intercessors for the Trier populace. It can be assumed that their graves were not left unprotected during the tumult of the 5th century and that they were in all likelihood guarded by pious men. They could have lived a communal existence which may be regarded as the foundation of the later monastery.

The large cemetery building was preceded by several periods of various large burial houses and funerary structures of which smaller segments were preserved in the new cemetery building. The burial chambers on the north side of the funerary hall were presumably the private mausoleums of privileged families or clans. Later construction has prevented an examination of the entire cemetery.

Inneres des Coemeterialgebäudes auf dem Nordfriedhof
Interior of the cemetery building in the north cemetery

Das Bild zeigt das Innere des Bestattungsgebäudes, wie es sich dem Besucher im beginnenden 5. Jh. dargeboten haben könnte. Beim Ausbau der letzten Phase, mit der Erweiterung nach Osten, wurden auch die drei Grabkammern mit den Bischofsgräbern inkorporiert. Ihre Gewölbe ragten etwa 0,40 m über den Fußboden des Gebäudes hinaus. Vermutlich hat man diese Erhöhung als Podium angelegt, das über zwei oder drei vorgebaute Treppenstufen zu erreichen war, vielleicht stand hier ein leichter Altar. Zu beiden Seiten dieses Podiums dürften die Abgänge zu den drei Kammern der Bischofsgräber gelegen haben. Da nur zwei der Kammern miteinander verbunden waren, war ein zweiter Abgang für die dritte Gruft erforderlich. Der gesamte übrige Raum war dicht mit Gräbern belegt, deren Ordnung nicht mehr erkennbar war. Die einzelnen Grabstätten, bei einigen ragte der Sarkophagdeckel aus der Erde, waren an ihren meist aus Marmor gefertigten Inschriftplatten, die häufig in Grabsteine aus Buntsandstein, zum Teil auch in gemauerte Sockel eingelegt waren, zu erkennen.

Die Wandgestaltung beruht auf Resten der Dekorationsmalerei, welche an der Südseite des Bauwerks beobachtet werden konnten. Die Rekonstruktion versucht, dem Betrachter eine Vorstellung über eine seltene, uns nicht mehr bekannten Bestattungsart zu verschaffen.

The picture shows the interior of the funerary structure as it might have appeared to a visitor at the beginning of the 5th century. The three crypts with the bishops' graves were incorporated during construction of the last phase, an extension to the east. The vaulting of the crypts extended about 16 in/40 cm above the floor of the building. Presumably this elevation was used as a dais to be reached by two or three steps in front of it; perhaps a light-weight altar stood there. The stairs to the three chambers with the bishops' graves were located probably on either side of the platform. As only two of the chambers were connected, a second descent became necessary for the third crypt. The entire rest of the space was crowded with graves, ordered in a form no longer recognizable. The individual graves - some of the sarcophagus lids extended above the earthen floor - could be recognized by the inscriptions, normally in marble, placed in a recess in burial stones of red sandstone or mounted on a masonry base. The wall decoration is based on remains of ornamental paintings observed on the interior of the south side of the building. The reconstruction attempts to give the viewer an idea of an uncommon burial practice no longer familiar to us.

Christogramm für eine Fünfzehnjährige
Christogram for a fifteen-year-old girl

Christogramm zwischen Alpha und Omega sowie zwei palmzweighaltenden Tauben
Christogram between alpha and omega and two doves holding palm branches

Grabstein der AMANDA
Gravestone for AMANDA

Lambert Dahm 05

St. Maximin, Inneres des Coemeterialgebäudes als Kirche
St. Maximin's, interior of the cemetery building after its conversion to a church

Der Baubefund ist dem auf Abb. 13 aus dem 5. Jh. fast gleich. Verändert hat sich lediglich der Ostteil durch den Einbau der Schola cantorum (an Stelle des Ambo) und den Anbau einer kleinen Apsis. Die freigelegten Reste des Ambo aus dem 6. Jh. bestärken die Vermutung, daß der Wandel vom reinen Bestattungsbau zur Kirche im 6. Jh. erfolgte. Die Umwandlung könnte im Zusammenhang mit der angeblichen Wiederherstellung von Maximin durch Bischof Nicetius (526/27-566) stehen. Es ist anzunehmen, daß bereits in spätrömischer, frühchristlicher Zeit Gottesdienste hier abgehalten wurden. Der Einbau der Schola cantorum (Sängerbühne) erfolgte im späten 8. Jh. nach der Aufgabe des Ambos.

Die weitestgehend erhaltene Wanddekoration dürfte unverändert geblieben sein, lediglich der unterste Teil, unmittelbar über dem Fußboden, war durch die Erhöhung des Bodens verdeckt. Diese Erhöhung entstand wohl durch die Überdeckung der alten Gräber mit einer Schicht neuer Gräber. Der Altar dürfte über den Gräbern der Bischöfe gestanden haben.

Die Rekonstruktion der Schola cantorum ist angelehnt an noch vorhandene Befunde in Rom, so zum Beispiel in St. Clemente. Mit dieser Rekonstruktion ist das Bild einer frühen Kirche entwickelt worden, deren Bedeutung einst weit über Trier hinaus ging.

St. Maximin als Mehrzweckhalle (Turnhalle, Konzertsaal, Festaula)
St. Maximin's as all-purpose hall (gymnasium, concert hall, festival hall)

The structure itself is almost the same as in illustration 13 (5th century). Only the east section has been altered by the construction of a *schola cantorum* (in place of the ambo) and the addition of a small apse. The excavated remains of the ambo from the 6th century underscore the assumption that the transformation from a purely funerary structure to a church occurred in the 6th century. This transformation may have been the reputed restoration of St. Maximin's by Bishop Nicetius (526/527-566). It is assumed that, as early as in the Late Roman, Early Christian period, worship services were held here. The installation of a *schola cantorum* (platform for singers) occurred in the late 8th century after the ambo was given up.

The greatest part of the preserved wall decoration probably remained unchanged; only the lower section, directly above the floor level, was covered when the floor level was raised. This occurred most likely when the old graves were covered with a layer of new graves. The altar stood more than likely over the graves of the bishops.

The reconstruction of the *schola cantorum* is based on extant remains in Rome, for example in San Clemente. This reconstruction can recreate an early church whose significance once reached far beyond Trier.

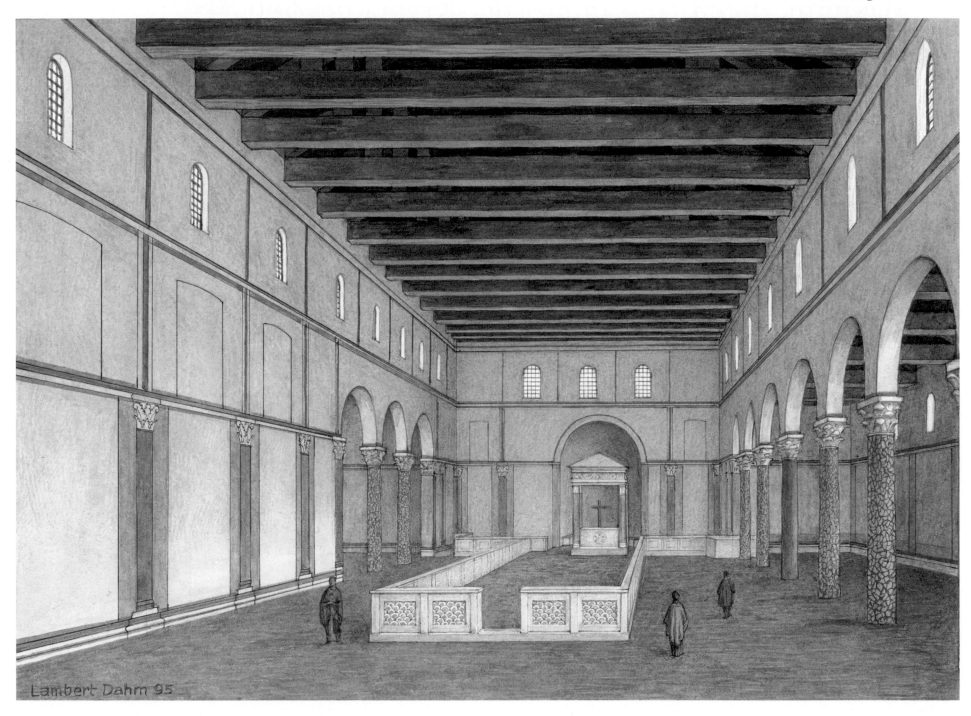

St. Maximin, die Mittelkammer der Krypta um 500
St. Maximin, the middle chamber of the crypt, around 500

Im späten 4. Jh. wurden, wie bei Abb. 13 erwähnt, im Osten des Coemeterialgebäudes drei Grabkammern inkorporiert. Zwei dieser Kammern waren miteinander verbunden und hatten einen gemeinsamen Zugang, während für die dritte ein eigener Zugang nötig war. Die Treppenabgänge sind platzbedingt zu beiden Seiten des Podiums anzunehmen. In der mittleren Kammer wird die Grabstätte des hl. Maximin vermutet. Wie diese Grabkammer um das Jahr 500 ausgesehen haben könnte, versucht diese Rekonstruktion darzustellen. Das große, innen und außen marmorverkleidete Grab war gemauert und wohl mit einem sarkophagähnlichen Deckel abgedeckt. Die nur geringen Marmorreste der äußeren Grabverkleidung führten zu der vorgelegten Lösung. Im Ostteil waren die Wände des Raumes bis zum Grab mit Kalksteinplatten verkleidet. Mit dem gleichen Material wurde auch der Fußboden ausgelegt. Die in situ gefundenen Reste des Fußbodens inspirierten zu dem hier gezeigten Wechsel. In dieser Kammer soll später auch Bischof Nicetius bestattet worden sein. An der Decke des Raumes (Tonne) konnten die Reste von zwei aufgemalten Quadratfeldern mit Kreiszier gesichert werden, die wohl zur Erstausstattung der Kammer gehörten. Trotz ihrer mehrmaligen Übermalung reichten die Reste zur Grundlage der Farbrekonstruktion. Bei der Westwand (Stirnseite) wurden Malereireste anderer im Bereich von St. Maximin gefundener Grabkammern mit floralen Ziermotiven, die sehr beliebt waren, als Vorbild genommen.

As mentioned in the text to illustration 13, three burial chambers were incorporated into the east end of the cemetery building in the late 4th century. Two of these chambers were connected and had a common access, whereas the third required its own access. It can be assumed that, for structural reasons, the descending stairs were located on either side of the dais. The postulated burial place of Maximinus is the middle chamber. The reconstruction attempts to present the burial chamber as it might have appeared around 500. The large tomb, lined with marble on the interior and exterior, was of masonry and probably covered with a lid similar to that on a sarcophagus. The few marble remains of the exterior covering led to the present reconstruction. In the east, the walls of the room were covered with limestone tiles, as was the floor. The remains of the floor found in situ inspired the alternating pattern shown here. Bishop Nicetius is said to have later also been buried in this chamber. The remains of two painted square fields with decorative circles were observed on the vaulted ceiling of the room, without doubt a feature in the first furnishings of the chamber. Despite having been painted over several times, the remains were sufficient to form the basis of the color reconstruction. For the west wall, remains of a popular decorative floral pattern from other burial chambers found in the area of St. Maximin's were used as a model.

Römische Familiengruft mit Sarkophagen. Treppenzugang im Bildvordergrund
Roman family mausoleum with coffins. Stairs in picture foreground

Maximinsarkophag. Von links nach rechts: Sündenfall, Guter Hirte, drei Jünglinge im Feuerofen
Maximinus sarcophagus. Left to right: Adam and Eve, Good Shepherd, the three men in the fiery furnace

Lambert Dahm 1995

St. Maximin, die Mittelkammer der Krypta um 900
St. Maximin's, the middle chamber of the crypt, around 900

Nur kurz nach dem Normanneneinfall (882) entstand wohl im letzten Jahrzehnt des 9. Jhs. diese einmalige Malerei. Soweit feststellbar, hatte die Kammer in den 400 Jahren der Zwischenzeit verschiedene Umgestaltungen erfahren. Dies läßt sich insbesondere an der Deckenwölbung (Tonne) ablesen, welche neben der spätrömischen die Reste verschiedener späterer Fassungen erkennen läßt, darunter zumindest auch eine mit figürlichen Darstellungen. Die Grabkammer ist zu einer Art Kapelle umgestaltet. Vor der Westwand (Stirnwand) wurde ein Sarkophag aufgestellt, an dessen Ostseite sich ein gemauerter Altar anschloß. Der Sarkophag war durch eine Verkleidung verdeckt, deren Brüstung rechts und links des Altares sichtbar war. Sie war gleich der Stirnwand und Teilen der Tonne mit figürlichen Malereien in Frescotechnik geziert, die eine starke Verwandtschaft zu den Buchmalereien der Zeit aufweisen. Die Stirnwand zeigte eine Kreuzigungsgruppe, während in der Tonne die vier Evangelisten zwischen stehenden Propheten dargestellt waren. Auf den Brüstungsteilen neben dem Altar waren Märtyrer und Märtyrerinnen mit Palmzweigen in den Händen abgebildet. Von der Tonnenmalerei waren beiderseits nur noch geringe Teile erkennbar, ihre Ausdehnung ist nicht bekannt. Der Westteil der Kammer wurde im 10. Jh. durch ein Fundament der ottonischen Kirche abgemauert, wodurch wohl auch die Malereischäden zu erklären sind.

This unique painting was created just shortly after the Viking invasion (882), probably in the last decade of the 9th century. As far as can be determined, the chamber had undergone different transformations in the intervening 400 years, especially visible on the vaulted ceiling. Along with the Late Roman decorations, the remains of different later decorations were visible, among them at least one pattern with figures. The chamber was remodeled into a kind of chapel. A sarcophagus was placed in front of the west wall. A projecting lower wall, a stone revetment, hid the sarcophagus, with the wall visible on either side of a masonry altar built in front of the sarcophagus. The lower wall, like the upper wall and parts of the vaulting, was ornamented with figures painted in the fresco technique, figures displaying a strong resemblance to book illuminations of that period. The upper wall shows a crucifixion group, whereas the four Evangelists between standing prophets are portrayed on the vaulting. Martyrs, men and women with palm branches in their hands, are represented on the lower wall to the left and right of the altar. Only small portions of the vaulting paintings were recognizable on either side; their extent is not known. In the 10th century, the west section of the chamber was walled up by a foundation of the Ottonian church, an credible explanation for the damage to the painting.

Grabung im südlichen Seitenschiff 1985
Excavations in south aisle in 1985

Gewölbeansatz der Familiengruft mit Treppenstufen
Vaulting of the family crypt with stairs

Lambert Dahm 1995

St. Maximin, die ottonische Kirche in der zweiten Hälfte des 10. Jhs.
St. Maximin's, the Ottonian church in the second half of the 10th century

Der Rekonstruktionsversuch mit Blick von Südwesten zeigt eine dreischiffige Basilika mit betontem Westbau. Der Kirchenneubau erfolgte wohl bald nach 934 und ist in drei Phasen verlaufen. So wurden der Ostbau 942, der Westbau 949 und die zweigeschossige Außenkrypta 952 geweiht. Die Dreiturmfassade zeigt in der Mittelachse eine breite Portalnische.

Dem Westbau war ein Atrium vorgelagert, das von jeweils zwei vorspringenden seitlichen Treppentürmen flankiert war, die in das zweite Obergeschoß des Atriums geführt haben könnten. Das Mittelschiff endete nach Osten, wie auch die beiden Seitenschiffe, mit einer Chorapsis, an die sich der niedere Bau der Außenkrypta anschloß.

Die Treppentürme zu beiden Seiten der Seitenschiffe führten zu Obergeschoßkapellen. Die ottonische Bausubstanz ist stellenweise noch bis in eine Höhe von 9 m im Mauerwerk der heutigen Kirche erhalten und beinhaltet die Reste von vier Fenstern der ottonischen Kirche, wovon eines fast ganz erhalten ist. Der ottonische Kirchenbau blieb ohne größere Veränderungen bis in das 13. Jh. bestehen, ehe ein Brand die Bauanlage zerstörte.

Die Rekonstruktion fußt auf den Untersuchungen und Unterlagen von A. Neyses. Sie zeigt einen interessanten Kirchenbau des 10. Jhs., der wahrscheinlich Vorbild für ähnliche Anlagen mit Außenkrypten war.

Heutige Ansicht der Kirchenanlage St. Maximin von Nordwesten
St. Maximin's today from the northwest

The reconstruction attempt with a view from the southwest shows a basilica of three aisles with a prominent west section. The building of the new church occurred probably soon after 934 and was conducted in three phases. The east section was consecrated in 942, the west section in 949, and the two-story outside crypt in 952. The front with three towers has a wide central porch niche.

An atrium opened in front of the west façade, flanked by two projecting side stair towers which could have led into the third story of the atrium building. Like the two side aisles, the nave ended on the east with a choir apse, to which the lower structure of the outside crypt was attached. The stair towers on either side of the aisles led to upper-story chapels. In some places, the fabric of the Ottonian building still rises to a height of 30 ft/9 m in the masonry of the present-day church and contains the remains of four windows from the Ottonian church, one of which is almost completely preserved. This Ottonian church stood without larger alterations until into the 13th century, when a fire destroyed the complex.

The reconstruction is based on the investigations and documentation by A. Neyses. It shows an interesting church of the 10th century that presumably served as a model for similar complexes with outside crypts.

Lambert Dahm 1995

St. Matthias, der romanische Bau mit den Abteigebäuden
Church of St. Matthias, the Romanesque structure with the abbey buildings

St. Matthias (ursprünglich St. Eucharius) ist eng mit dem Südfriedhof verbunden. Durch die Bestattung der ersten Trierer Bischöfe Eucharius, Valerius im späten 3. Jh. und, im frühen 4. Jhd., Maternus wurde der Südfriedhof, wie bezeugt, durch das Grab des hl. Eucharius zu einem Ort der Verehrung. Über die Lage ihrer Gräber ist nichts bekannt. Bischof Cyrillus ließ im Jahre 454 an Stelle der zerstörten Grabkapelle eine neue Grabkirche errichten, die spätestens beim Normanneneinfall 882 zerstört wurde. Etwa 100 Jahre später wurde mit einem Neubau begonnen, der abermals 100 Jahr

später (1127) einer neu erbauten größeren Kirche, die 1148 durch Papst Eugen III. (1145-1153) geweiht wurde, weichen mußte. Bei diesen Neubauarbeiten wurden auch die Reliquien des Apostels Matthias wieder aufgefunden. Die Abbildung zeigt die romanische Kirche, wie sie etwa um 1200 ausgesehen haben könnte. Die ersten Veränderungen haben bereits in frühgotischer Zeit begonnen, denen weitere in den nächsten Jahrhunderten folgten. Südlich der Kirche lagen die Klostergebäude. Die Klostergründung soll bis in das 6. Jh. zurückreichen, für das Jahr 707 ist das Kloster durch eine Urkunde bezeugt. Die frühen Anlagen sind unbekannt, auch vom romanischen Kloster (um 1000) ist nichts oberirdisch erhalten. Untersuchungen ergaben, daß seine Ausmaße denen der Anlage des frühen 13. Jhs. entsprachen.

St. Matthias's (originally St. Eucharius's) is closely associated with the south Roman cemetery. As is documented, owing to the interment of the first Trier bishops, Eucharius and Valerius, in the late 3rd century, and Maternus (?) in the early 4th century, the south cemetery was a place of veneration, especially because of the grave of St. Eucharius. Nothing is known about the location of the graves. In 454, Bishop Cyrillus had a new burial church built on the spot of the destroyed burial chapel. This new church was destroyed, at the latest, during the Viking invasion in 882. About 100 years later a new building was begun, which, again 100 years later (1127), was replaced by a newly built larger church, consecrated by Pope Eugene III (1145-1153) in 1148. During this new construction, the relics of the Apostle Matthias were rediscovered. The picture shows the Romanesque church as it might have appeared around 1200. The first alterations had begun in the early Gothic period, followed by others in the ensuing centuries. The monastic structures were located on the south side of the church. It is said that the monastery founding dates back to the 6th century; the first written record dates from 707. Nothing is known of the early structures, nor is anything of the Romanesque building (about 1000) preserved above ground. Investigations have shown that its dimensions corresponded to those of the Gothic complex from the early 13th century.

St. Matthias von Südosten mit Benediktinerabtei. Pfeil rechts: Quirinuskapelle über der Albanagruft im Friedhof
St. Matthias's from southeast with Benedictine Abbey. Arrow right: Quirinus Chapel above Albana mausoleum in the cemetery

Lambert Dahm 01

Die Abteikirche St. Matthias um 1350
The Abbey Church of St. Matthias around 1350

Das Bild zeigt die Kirche, wie sie wohl um die Mitte des 14. Jhs. aussah. Die hier dargestellte frühgotische Turmform von 1320 entstand im Zusammenhang mit einer Totalerneuerung der Dachstühle zu Beginn des 14. Jahrhunderts. Der dargestellte Turmhelm wurde um 1480 durch einen Doppelhelmturm ersetzt, dem zwischen 1714 und 1719 eine barocke Fassung folgte. Die heutige Turmform entstand nach einem schweren Feuer im Jahre 1783, das die Dächer, Turmhelme und auch den Glockenstuhl zerstörte. Völlig neu ist die heutige klassizistische Bekrönung nach dem Entwurf des Trierer Baumeisters Anton Neurohr aus dem Jahre 1786, deren endgültige Fertigstellung im Jahr 1886 erfolgte.

Die Westfassade gliedert sich in zwei Zonen, deren untere durch das Portal und die Fenster belebt wurde. Durch einen Konsolenfries getrennt, beginnt die Giebelzone. Ihr Mittelfeld wird durch drei Blendarkaden aufgelöst, von deren Kapitellen sich eine profilierte Leiste nach außen fortsetzt und so die Verbindung zu den übrigen Zierelementen herstellt. Auf dieser Giebelzone ruht der Turm.

Rechts neben der Kirche schließt sich das Quadrum des Klosters aus der ersten Hälfte des 13. Jhs. an. Dieser Klosterbereich mit der Klausur war durch eine Mauer abgeschirmt. An der linken Seite des Kirchenvorhofes standen die Gebäude zur Versorgung der Pilger, die neben Herberge und Brunnenhaus noch weitere Gebäude, einschließlich Torhaus, umfaßten.

The picture shows the church as it might have appeared around the middle of the 14th century. The early Gothic tower from 1320 presented here was constructed during a total renewal of the roof at the beginning of the 14th century. The helm roof of the tower was replaced by a double helm roof around 1480, which in turn was replaced by a baroque crown between 1714 and 1719. The present form of the tower was created after a devastating fire in 1783 which destroyed the roofs, helm roof and the belfry. The present-day neo-classical corona was built completely new according to a design by the Trier city architect Anton Neurohr in 1786, but was fully finished only in 1886.

The west façade is divided into two zones, the lower of which is enhanced by the portal and the windows. A console-like stringcourse separates the lower part from the beginning of the gable zone, enlivened in the middle by three blind arcades. From their capitals, another stringcourse continues to the outside and creates the connection to the rest of the ornamentation. The tower stands above this gable zone.

St. Matthias und neugestalteter Freihof mit Brunnen und Pacellikreuz
St. Matthias's and the newly designed courtyard with fountain and Pacelli Cross

Die drei ersten Trierer Bischöfe Valerius, Eucharius, Maternus v.l.n.r
Left to right: the first three Trier Bishops Valerius, Eucharius, Maternus

The quadrangle of the monastery cloister structure from the first half of the 13th century adjoins the church on the right. This closed area of the monastery with its cloister was protected by a wall. The buildings for pilgrims stand on the left side of the church courtyard, consisting of lodgings and well, but also other facilities, including a gatehouse.

50

Die Matthiaskirche von Nordosten gesehen
St. Matthias's seen from the north

Dieser Blick bot sich dem Betrachter von der Heiligkreuzer Höhe um 1520. Der Westturm der Kirche bekam etwa um 1480 diesen Doppelhelm. Er ist auf den beiden Stadtansichten von S. Münster (1548) und M. Merian (1646) deutlich zu erkennen. Diese Helmform löste den schlanken Turm aus der ersten Hälfte des 14. Jhs. (Abb. 19) ab. Über die Umstände der Errichtung ist nichts überliefert. Die Datierung dieser Doppelhelmform um 1480 ist durch die Darstellung auf einem Schlußstein im spätgotischen Gewölbe, das um 1500 erbaut wurde, gesichert.

Der römische Südfriedhof, in dessen Bereich St. Matthias steht, weist eine ähnliche Vielfalt an Begräbnisstätten, einschließlich der Grabkammern und Grüfte, auf wie der Nordfriedhof. Allerdings sind hier im Süden bisher keine Coemeterialbauten nachweisbar, wie sie in St. Maximin ergraben wurden, obwohl auch hier im Süden Kapellen über Grabkammern errichtet wurden, die dabei meist zerstört wurden. Sie lagen zum Teil vor der hier dargestellten Nordseite der Kirche. Grabungsbefunde lassen vermuten, daß die Gräber der Bischöfe Eucharius und Valerius sowie ihre von Bischof Cyrillus im 5. Jh. neu erbaute Grabkirche (Text Abb. 18) im Bereich unter dem südlichen Seitenschiff der späteren Kirche lagen.

The observer would have been given this view of the church, for example, from Holy Cross Hill around 1520. Around 1480, the double helm roof was erected on the west tower of the church, clearly visible on the two engraved views of Trier by Sebastian Münster (1548) and Matthew Merian (1646).
The double helm roof replaced the slender spire from the first half of the 14th century (illustration 19). No documentation exists on the circumstances of the construction. The dating of around 1480 for the double helm is confirmed by the picture of the church on a keystone in the Late Gothic vaulting, which was built around 1500.
The south Roman cemetery, where St. Matthias's stands, exhibits a similar diversity of burial sites, including burial chambers and tombs, as in the north cemetery. However, no cemetery buildings have been documented in the south as were excavated in St. Maximin's, although chapels were erected over mausoleums, most of which have been destroyed. Some were located in front of the north side of the church, pictured here. Burial finds suggest that the graves of the Bishops Eucharius and Valerius as well as the new burial church (text, illustration 18) built by Bishop Cyrillus in the 5th century were located under the south aisle of the later church.

Blick auf St. Matthias über die Heiligkreuzer Höhe vom Petrisberg
View of St. Matthias's over Holy Cross Hill from Petrisberg Mountain

St. Paulin, Rekonstruktion der romanischen Kirche des 11. und 12. Jhs.
St. Paulin's, reconstruction of the Romanesque church from the 11th and 12th centuries

Diese Kirche ersetzte die Basilika des Bischofs Felix aus der Zeit um 390, die 1093 einer Brandkatastrophe zum Opfer fiel. Die Arbeiten für den Neubau wurden schon bald, noch im 11. Jh., aufgenommen. Im wesentlichen entstand das Bauwerk in der ersten Hälfte des 12. Jhs., so daß die Kirche am 31. Januar 1148 durch Papst Eugen III. (1145-1153) geweiht werden konnte. Sie war über 500 Jahre in Benutzung, ehe sie im Jahre 1674, gleich St. Maximin, von den Franzosen durch Sprengung zerstört wurde.

Das in der Kirchenachse auf dem westlichen Kirchenvorplatz stehende Immunitätskreuz wurde um das Jahr 1088 errichtet, wie die Inschrift auf dem Kreuz besagt. Das Bild versucht eine Situation um das Jahr 1200 wiederzugeben. Die Rekonstruktion der Kirche fußt im wesentlichen auf einer Zeichnung des Kanonikus Oehmbs aus dem Jahre 1792, welche die Kirche des 11. und 12. Jahrhunderts zeigt. In groben Zügen wird das Aussehen der Kirche auf den Stadtansichten von S. Münster und M. Merian bestätigt, soweit die dortige minimale Größe als Zeugnis gelten darf.

St. Paulin war eine Stiftskirche. Bereits in fränkische Zeit

St. Paulin: Turmhöhe und Kirchenschiffslänge sind gleich
St. Paulin's: height of tower and length of nave are the same

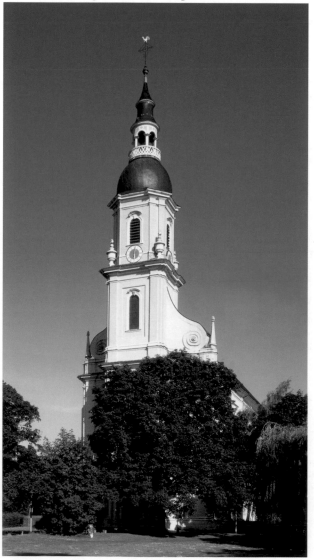

St. Paulin und alter Friedhof von Südwesten
St. Paulin's and the old cemetery from the southwest

hatte sich hier ein Priesterkollegium gebildet, das später zum Kollegiatstift erhoben wurde und bis zum Jahre 1802 bestand. Das klosterähnlich mit einem Kreuzgang angelegte zerstörte Stiftsgebäude lag südlich der Kirche und ist hier auf der rechten Bildseite nur noch im Ansatz zu sehen.

This church replaced the basilica built under Bishop Felix around 390, which was destroyed by fire in 1093. The work on the new building was begun very soon, as early as in the 11th century. The structure was essentially completed in the first half of the 12th century, so that the church could be consecrated by Pope Eugene III on January 31, 1148. It was in use for over 500 years, when, in 1674, it was blown up by the French, as was St. Maximin's.

Symbolizing jurisdiction, the cross, standing aligned with the central axis of the church, was erected west of it around 1088, as is stated on the cross. The picture attempts to portray the scene from around 1200, with the reconstruction of the church based in essence on a drawing by Canon Oehmbs from 1792, showing the church of the 11th and 12th centuries. In general, the appearance of the church is confirmed by the engraved views of Trier by S. Münster and M. Merian, as far as the small size can be valid documentation.

St. Paulin's was the church of a collegiate foundation. As early as the Frankish period, a community of priests had been established there and later raised to the rank of collegiate foundation, existing until 1802. The monastery-like collegiate building, also destroyed, was laid out with a cloister annexed on the south side of the church. It can be seen in part on the right side of the picture.

Lambert Dahm 1996

St. Irminen im 13. Jh.
St. Irmina's in the 13th century

Wie auf diesem Bild könnte die romanische Kirche von St. Irminen um die Mitte des 13. Jhs. ausgesehen haben. Sie wurde im rechten Winkel in den nördlichen Teil der östlichen Horreahalle eingebaut, reichte aber nach ihrer Erweiterung im 11. Jh. mit ihrem Langhaus, an das sich das Querschiff mit den drei Apsiden und dem Turm anschloß, mehr als zur Hälfte über die Horreahalle nach Osten hinaus. Auf dem Bild erkennt man die wohl bei der frühen Klosteranlage mitverwendete östliche Mauer der Osthalle der Horrea mit ihren typischen Arkaden. Es ist anzunehmen, daß zu dieser Zeit nur Teile der römischen Halle benutzt wurden, die den räumlichen Bedürfnissen des Klosters entsprechend umgestaltet waren. Der Kirchturm aus dem 11. Jh., hier in seiner ursprünglichen Form dargestellt, wurde erst im 17. Jh. aufgestockt. Sein heutiges klassizistisches Obergesims erhielt er nach einem Brand im Jahre 1836. Rechts neben der Irminenkirche erkennt man die aus dem 12. Jh. stammende Pauluskirche, die bis zum Ende des 18. Jhs. bestand und im Bereich des heutigen Irminenfreihofes lag. Auf der rechten Bildseite (unter dem Baum) ist die sogenannte Modestakapelle zu erkennen, die wahrscheinlich noch aus merowingischer Zeit stammte. Sie soll die Begräbnisstätte der ersten Äbtissin von St. Irminen, Modesta (7. Jh.), gewesen sein. Die Kapelle, durch einen Flur mit der romanischen Kirche verbunden, wurde 1809 abgebrochene.

Blick von Westen auf St. Irminen. Pfeil: aufgestockter Kirchturm
View from the west toward St. Irmina's. Arrow: raised church tower

The Romanesque Church of St. Irmina could have appeared in the mid-13th century as depicted here. It was built at a right angle into the north section of the east *horrea* hall, one of the Roman food storehouses. Following its expansion in the 11th century, the nave stretched more than halfway across the *horrea* hall to the east, expanded further by the transept with three apses and the tower. On the left, the picture shows the east wall of the east hall of the *horrea* with its typical arcades, presumably already integrated into the early convent. It may be assumed that, at that time, only parts of the Roman hall were in use, altered to correspond to the needs of the convent. The church tower from the 11th century, shown here in its original form, was not raised until the 17th century. The present-day neo-classical upper section was added after a fire in 1836. St. Paul's from the 12th century is visible next to the Irmina Church on the right. Until the end of the 18th century, it stood in this form on the grounds of St. Irmina's convent yard. The so-called Modesta Chapel, probably dating from the Merovingian period, stands on the right side of the picture (under the tree). The first Abbess of St. Irmina's, Modesta (7th century), is said to have been buried there. The chapel, connected to the Romanesque church by a hallway, was torn down in 1809.

Die Abtei St. Martin um 1490
St. Martin's Abbey around 1490

Auch diese ehemalige Benediktinerabtei entwickelte sich aus frühchristlichen Anfängen. Ausgangspunkt war wohl eine suburbane römische Villa, die nach der Schenkung an die Christengemeinde zum Teil zur Kirche gewandelt wurde. Neben anderen Funden wurde auch eine Anzahl von Sarkophaggräbern mit Bestattungen aus dem 4. und 5. Jh. freigelegt. Nach der Überlieferung soll bereits im 6. Jh. eine dem hl. Martin von Tours geweihte Kirchen erbaut worden sein, womit die Kontinuität auch in fränkischer Zeit gesichert sein dürfte. Wahrscheinlich hat sich bei den Kirchen auch eine klösterliche Niederlassung befunden, aus der dann später die Benediktinerabtei hervor ging. Wie alle Trierer Klöster hatte auch St. Martin ein wechselhaftes Schicksal. Am Ende des 11. Jh. entstand eine neue, die romanische, Kirche, ein Ersatz für die durch Brand zerstörte Vorgängerkirche. Das Bild versucht, den Zustand von Kirche und Abtei in der Zeit um 1490 wiederzugeben. Zentrales Bauwerk der Anlage war die Kirche. Der Abteibereich, der außerhalb der Stadtmauer lag, hatte eine eigene Einfriedung mit einem Tor zur Mosel und den Mühlen hin. Das Kloster lag nördlich der Kirche und bestand aus mehreren Gebäuden, die zum Teil mit Treppentürmen ausgestattet waren. Die Lage des für das Kloster wichtigen Kreuzganges ist nicht bekannt. Die Mühlen im Vordergrund, einst Eigentum des Erzbischofs, dann im Besitz der Abtei, kamen 1474 durch einen entsprechenden Vertrag in den Besitz der Stadt.

This former Benedictine abbey also developed from Early Christian beginnings. The starting point was apparently a suburban Roman villa which was partially converted into a church after it had been donated to the Christian community. A number of sarcophagus burials from the 4th and 5th centuries were unearthed along with other finds. According to tradition, a church dedicated to St. Martin of Tour was built as early as the 6th century, demonstrating continuity also during the Frankish period. A monastic community likely existed next to the church, from which the Benedictine abbey later developed. Like all Trier monasteries and convents, St. Martin's experienced a tumultuous history. At the end of the 11th century, a new church was built in Romanesque style as a replacement for the previous church, destroyed by fire. The picture attempts to reproduce the appearance of the church and abbey from the time around 1490. The church was the center of the complex. The abbey itself, outside the city wall, had its own enclosure with a gate to the Moselle, leading to the mills. The monastery was located north of the church and comprised several structures, some of which were equipped with stair towers. The location of the cloister, so important for the abbey, is unknown. The mills in the foreground, once owned by the archbishop, then by the abbey, were taken over by the city through an agreement in 1474.

St. Martin vor der alten Stadtmauer. Pfeil: heutiges Studentenwohnheim
St. Martin's outside the old city wall. Arrow: student dormitory today

Das Martinskloster. Pfeil: spätgotische Kreuzigungsgruppe
St. Martin's Abbey. Arrow: late Gothic crucifixion group

Lambert Dahm 1996

Kloster St. Agneten und der Bereich der Kaiserthermen um 1450
Convent of St. Agnes and the area of the former Imperial Baths around 1450

Das Areal und die Reste der Kaiserthermen (oder des Kaiserpalastes) wurden auch im Mittelalter genutzt. Über die Nutzung aus der unmittelbar nachrömischen Zeit ist nichts bekannt. Vom 5. bis zum 11. Jh. sollen Familien des Stadtadels ihr Wohnquartier hier bezogen haben. Im 12. Jh., unter Erzbischof Bruno (1102-1124), wurden sie (bis ins 19. Jh.) in die Stadtbefestigung einbezogen. Dabei wurde das untere östliche Fenster der Südapsis des Caldariums als Stadttor, die sogenannte Altport, genutzt. Die Stadtmauer schloß sich zu beiden Seiten an die Thermenruine an. Im Bereich der ehemaligen Palaestra stand die alte Pfarrkirche St. Gervasius, die wahrscheinlich im späten 11. Jh. erbaut wurde.

Hinter der Kirche ist die Klosteranlage von St. Agneten mit ihrer nach Norden liegenden, das Kloster leicht überragenden Kirche zu sehen. Wahrscheinlich im frühen

13. Jh. gegründet, wird das Kloster in der Mitte des 15. Jhs. von Augustinerinnen übernommen. Im frühen 18. Jh. entstand ein barocker Neubau, der später zur preußischen Kaserne umfunktioniert und danach ein Wohnquartier wurde, das den Krieg 1939/45 nicht überlebte. Das vorgelegte Bild zeigt einen möglichen Zustand um 1450. Der Bach im Vordergrund des Bildes ist eine Abzweigung des Olewiger Baches, der sogenannte Stadtbach, der wenig weiter westlich zur Weberbach hin floß und von dort weiter durch die Stadt.

The grounds as well as the remains of the Imperial Baths (or Imperial Palace) were also used in the Middle Ages. Nothing is known, however, about their use immediately after the Roman period. It is said that families of the city's nobility lived there from the 5th to the 11th century. In the 12th century, under Archbishop Bruno (1102-1124), the remains were integrated into the city wall (until into the 19th century). The lower east window of the south apse of the caldarium (warm bath) functioned as a city gate, the so-called Altport (Old Gate). The city wall adjoined both sides of the ruin. The first parish church of St. Gervasius, probably erected in the late 11th century, stood in the area of the former sports grounds.

Behind the church, the Convent of St. Agnes is visible with its church further north, rising slightly higher than the convent buildings. Founded presumably in the 13th century, the convent was taken over by Augustinian nuns in the 15th century. In the early 18th century, a new church was built in baroque style, later secularized by the French and converted into a Prussian barracks, then into socialized housing which did not survive World War II. The reconstruction picture shows a possible state around 1450. The brook in the picture foreground is a branch of the Olewig Brook, the so-called city brook, which flowed on as the Weavers' Brook a bit further to the west and from there through the city.

Blick von Süden auf die heutige Ausgrabung. Pfeil links: Weberbach. Pfeil Mitte: Stadtbibliothek. Pfeil rechts: Palastgarten
View from the south toward the excavations today. Arrow left: Weberbach (street). Arrow center: City Library. Arrow right: Palace Garden

Lambert Dahm 1997

Simeonstift und die zur Simeonkirche umgebaute Porta Nigra, um 1100

Courtyard of Simeon's Collegiate Foundation with Porta Nigra as Simeon's Church, around 1100

Die Porta Nigra verdankt ihren guten Erhaltungszustand der Tatsache, daß Erzbischof Poppo von Babenberg (1016-1047) sie zur Doppelkirche ausbauen ließ. Anläßlich einer Pilgerfahrt des Erzbischofs nach Palästina lernte er Simeon kennen und brachte ihn mit nach Trier. Simeon errichtete wohl um 1030 im Ostturm der Porta Nigra eine Einsiedlerzelle, in der er bis zu seinem Tod 1035 lebte, er wurde dort auch beigesetzt. Auch der Erzbischof fand nach seinem Tod 1047 hier seine letzte Ruhe. Kurz nach dem Tod Simeons, 1035, ließ ihn Erzbischof Poppo heiligsprechen und zu seinen Ehren die Porta Nigra zur Kirche ausbauen. Die untere Kirche, im ersten Obergeschoß der Porta, war die Laienkirche, während die Kirche für die Stiftskleriker im zweiten Obergeschoß lag. Wohl um die gleiche Zeit gründete Poppo westlich neben der Porta ein Kanonikerstift, das Simeonstift. Das Stift war klosterähnlich im Geviert angelegt, mit allen Einrichtungen für eine solche Gemeinschaft. Zu den wichtigsten Bauteilen des Quadrums gehörte der Kreuzgang, der hier nicht im Erdgeschoß, sondern in Höhe der Unterkirche lag. Die Arkaden sind Unterbau für den Kreuzgang, der ehemals alle vier Seiten des Innenhofes umgab. Der Blick ist hier auf den Ostflügel und den Ostteil des Nordflügels gerichtet. An diesen

schloß das erhöhte Kapitelhaus an, welches an den Westturm der Porta Nigra angebaut war, aber leider nicht erhalten ist.

The Porta Nigra owes its good state of preservation to the fact that Archbishop Poppo of Babenberg (1016-1047) had it converted into a double church. On the occasion of his pilgrimage to Palestine, he became acquainted with Simeon and brought him back to Trier. Around 1030, Simeon established a hermit's cell in the east tower of the Porta Nigra, where he lived until his death in 1035; he was also buried in the gate. The Archbishop also found his last resting place there after his death in 1047. Shortly after Simeon's death, Archbishop Poppo initiated Simeon's canonization in 1035 and had the Porta Nigra converted into a church in Simeon's honor. The lower church, in the first window story of the Porta, was the lay church, whereas the church for the foundation's clergy was in the second window story. Around the same time, Poppo founded a college of canons, the Simeon's College to the west adjoining the Porta. The collegiate building was laid out like a monastery quadrangle with all the facilities for such a community. Among the most important elements of the quadrangle was the cloister, which was not on the ground floor but in the upper story on the level of the first church. The lower arcades were merely the supports for the cloister, which originally surrounded all four sides of the inner courtyard. The view in the picture looks toward the east wing and the east part of the north wing. The chapter house towered over this wing, adjoining on one side and connecting to the west tower of the Porta Nigra on the other side. Unfortunately, the chapter house has not survived.

Blick über den Innenhof auf die westliche Stadtseite der Porta Nigra
View across the courtyard toward the west side of the Porta Nigra facing the city

Luftaufnahme von Süden. Pfeil: Simeonstift
Aerial photo from the south. Arrow: St. Simeon's

Lambert Dahm 89

Rekonstruktion der Simeonkirche mit Simeonstor um 1370
Reconstruction of St. Simeon's Church with the Porta Nigra and St. Simeon's Gate around 1370

Leider gibt es von der Nordseite, der Landseite, keine zuverlässigen Bilder. Die bekannten Darstellungen sind in ihren Detailwiedergaben sehr unterschiedlich, oft gar unklar. Bei dieser Rekonstruktion ist die Porta Nigra unschwer als Kernbau der Doppelkirche zu erkennen. Die Verbindung zwischen antiker und christlicher Architektur schuf hier einen großartigen und einmaligen Baukomplex, wie er in keiner anderen Stadt anzutreffen war. Bestimmender Bauteil ist die Porta Nigra, deren Erdgeschoß durch Aufschüttung verdeckt ist. Diese ist durch eine starke Stützmauern begrenzt und diente dem Stift als Friedhof, zu dem wohl auch die beiden Kapellen gehörten. Der Zugang zum Friedhof, er wurde Bartholomäusfriedhof genannt, erfolgte durch ein zur Tür vergrößertes Fenster im unteren Seitenschiff (alter Wehrgang) der Porta, unmittelbar neben dem Westturm. Auf diesem Bild ist eine Situation nachempfunden, wie sie sich wenige Jahre vor dem Bau des Ramsdonkturmes dargeboten haben könnte. Unmittelbar an die Chorapsis der Kirchen, nach Osten hin, schloß sich das nördliche Stadttor, das Simeonstor, an, von dem aus die von der Mosel kommende Stadtmauer weiter nach Osten verlief. Nach Westen folgten an den Westturm der Porta Nigra die Gebäude des Stiftes, die sich harmonisch anfügten.

Die Porta Nigra von der Landseite gesehen. Pfeil: Simeonstift
The Porta Nigra seen from outside the city. Arrow: Simeon's College

Regrettably, there exist no reliable pictures of the north side, outside the city wall. The known depictions vary decidedly in their reproduction of details, some even unclear. This reconstruction clearly shows the Porta Nigra as the core of the double church. The union of ancient and Christian architecture created a magnificent and unique building complex not to be found in any other city. The determining construction element is the Porta Nigra, whose ground floor is hidden by an earthen wall reinforced by a thick retaining wall. This earthen area served the collegiate foundation as a cemetery, to which the two chapels presumably belonged. Access to the cemetery, called St. Bartholomew's Cemetery, was gained through a Roman window enlarged to make a doorway in the north side aisle (former sentry walkway) directly next to the west tower. This picture shows the site as it might have looked a few years before the Ramsdonk Tower (illustration 27) was erected. Directly adjacent to the east choir apse of the church stood the north city gate, St. Simeon's Gate, from where the city wall coming from the Moselle ran further to the east. To the west, the facilities of the collegiate foundation joined harmoniously onto the west tower of the Porta Nigra.

Lambert Dahm 1955

Der Befestigungsturm neben dem Simeonstor
The fortifications tower next to Simeon's Gate

Über den Standort und das Aussehen dieses etwa um 1389 entstandenen Befestigungsturmes, auch Ramsdonk genannt, gibt es keine authentischen Unterlagen. Die Frage nach dem Standort ist wahrscheinlich beantwortet, nachdem bei Kanalarbeiten im Sommer 1967 ein schweres, bis zu fünf Meter unter das heutige Straßenniveau reichendes Fundament aus Rotsandstein gefunden wurde. Dieses Fundament war wohl die Südwestecke des Turmes, der etwa zehn Meter weiter südlich und etwa sieben Meter weiter östlich als bisher angenommen stand. Damit ist auch die Annahme, daß der Turm jenseits des Stadtgrabens gestanden habe, nicht haltbar. Dies wird durch die Klage in einem Bericht des kaiserlichen Kommissars Erndlin bestätigt, der anläßlich einer Besichtigung nicht nahe genug an den Turm heran kam. Hätte der Turm vor dem Graben gestanden oder eine Tordurchfahrt gehabt, wäre Erndlin ohne Probleme näher an die Nordseite, um die es geht, gelangt. Erndlin schreibt von einem starken viereckigem Turm mit vier Absätzen (Stockwerke), der sich neben und über der St. Simeonpforte erhob. Danach war der Turm fünfgeschossig. Über dem zweiten Absatz an der Nordseite stand eine weitere gut mannshohe vergoldete Petrusfigur, ähnlich wie sie Erndlin auch über der Simeonpforte beschrieben hat. Das Schicksal des Turmes und seine Zerstörung sind unklar. Das Bild zeigt eine Situation, wie sie sich um 1500 hätte ergeben können.

No authentic records have survived concerning the position and the appearance of this fortifications tower, called Ramsdonk, erected around 1389. The question of position was likely answered after work on the sewer canal in 1967 unearthed a massive red sandstone foundation extending as much as 16 ft/5 m below the present street level. This foundation was presumably the southwest corner of the tower that stood about 33 ft/ 10 m further south and about 23 ft/7 m further east than had been assumed. This discovery no longer supports the supposition that the tower stood beyond the defense ditch. This fact is confirmed in the complaint in a report by the Imperial Commissioner Erndlin, who stated that in his inspection he could not approach close enough to the tower. Had the tower stood beyond the ditch or had it had a gateway, Erndlin would have been able to reach the north side, the side in question, without any problem. Erndlin writes of an enormous square tower of five stories which rose adjacent to and above St. Simeon's Gate. Above the second story, a life-sized, gilded statue of St. Peter stood on the north side, similar to the one Erndlin had described above Simeon's Gate. The fate of the tower and its destruction are unclear. The picture shows the site as it might have appeared around 1500.

Panoramablick auf Porta Nigra und Simeonstift. Simonstift rechts und Wohnhäuser links stehen auf den Stadtmauerfundamenten. Pfeil: Ramsdonk-Turmfundamente unter der heutigen Terrasse
Panoramic view of the Porta Nigra and Simeon's College. Simeon's College on the right and houses on the left built on the foundations of the city wall. Arrow: Ramsdonk Tower foundations under the present terrace

Lambert Dahm 98

Simeonkirche und Porta Nigra mit Umgebung um 1500
St. Simeon's Church (Porta Nigra) with its environs around 1500, seen from the south

Diese Rekonstruktion stützt sich weitgehend auf einen Stich Merians von 1646, die einzige verläßliche Darstellung. Kern der monumentalen Baugruppe ist die Porta Nigra, deren Erdgeschoß mit den Durchgangstoren für den Bau der Freitreppe zu den Kirchen zugeschüttet wurde. An den Ostturm der Porta wurde die Chorapsis (um 1150/1160) angebaut. Auf den erhaltene Westturm wurde der Glockenturm der romanischen Kirche aufgesetzt. Das Mittelschiff der Oberkirche erhob sich über die Mauerkrone des Zwingers der Porta Nigra. Der Eingang zur oberen Kirche war an den Westturm angebaut. Auf dem Bild erkennt man sehr gut die im Winkel erbaute Treppe mit Vordach über dem zum Eingang erweiterten Fenster im dritten Turmgeschoß. Links neben dem Westturm und dem Aufgang zur Oberkirche lag das Stift. Der Torbau mit den drei Bögen im Vordergrund war der Eingang zum Stiftsbering und über die Freitreppe zu den Kirchen. Neben der Treppe zur Oberkirche stand die Johanneskapelle, auf der rechten Seite der Freitreppe die 1287 geweihte Andreaskapelle. An die Chorapsis schloß sich nach Osten das nördliche Stadttor, das Simeontor, an. Dahinter der Befestigungsturm, der sogenannte Ramsdonkturm, wie bei Abb. 27, der 1389 zur Verstärkung des Simeontores erbaut wurde. Die Bürgerhäuser auf der rechten Straßenseite dürften gotischen Ursprungs sein und zeigen die gleiche Charakteristik, wie sie auch von anderen, noch bis zum Krieg erhaltenen gotischen Häuserreihen in Trier bekannt ist.

This reconstruction is based for the most part on an engraving by Matthew Merian from the mid-17th century, the only reliable depiction. The core of the monumental complex is the Porta Nigra; the ground floor of the Roman gatehouse was filled in to build the open stairs. The choir apse (around 1150/1160) was added to the east tower of the Porta, and the belfry tower of the Romanesque church was built atop the preserved west tower. The nave of the upper church rose above the top wall of the gatehouse. The entry to the upper church was built onto the west tower. Leading at a right angle up to the third story of the west tower, the stairs are covered by a roof over a window which was extended downward to form the entrance. The collegiate foundation building adjoined the west tower to the left of the stairs. The gate with the three arches in the foreground served as the entrance to the foundation enclosure and to the open stairs leading to the churches. St. John's Chapel stood next to the steps to the upper church; St. Andrew's Chapel, consecrated in 1287, stood to the right of the open stairs. The north city gate, St. Simeon's Gate, adjoined the choir to the east. Behind the gate stood the fortifications tower, the so-called Ramsdonk Tower, as in illustration 27, constructed in 1389 to reinforce St. Simeon's Gate. The townspeople's houses on the right side of the street were presumably Gothic houses and display the same architectural characteristics as other rows of Gothic houses known in Trier until World War II.

Porta Nigra - Stadtseite. In der Lücke über der heutigen Straße standen Tor und Ramsdonkturm
Porta Nigra - city side. The gate and the Ramsdonk Tower stood over the present street

Lambert Dahm 95

Die Basilika (Kaiseraula) und ihre Umgebung um die Mitte des 7. Jhs.
The "Basilika" (Imperial Throne Room) and its surroundings around the middle of the 7th century

Nach der Überlieferung soll der fränkische Gaugraf seinen Amtssitz im Bereich dieser römischen Anlage genommen haben. Die große Aula war nicht mehr benutzbar, es fehlten Dach und Fenster. Seit ihrer Fertigstellung zu Beginn des 4. Jhs. waren fast 350 Jahre vergangen, so daß Spuren der Verwitterung nahezu selbstverständlich waren, abgesehen von den Schäden durch die Ereignisse des 5. Jahrhunderts. Das Mauerwerk selbst, bis zu 2,70 m stark, war nahezu unzerstörbar.

Es ist davon auszugehen, daß die Unterkunft des Gaugrafen in einem der Seitentrakte lag, wobei die östlich der Aula gelegenen Gebäude am ehesten geeignet waren. Mittelpunkt der Anlage war ein Saal mit nach Süden liegender Apsis. Nördlich hinter diesem Saal lagen eine Eingangshalle und ein kleiner Innenhof, der wahrscheinlich nach Norden und Osten von kleineren Räumen umgeben war. Die Annahme, daß auch die Vorhalle der Aula durch die Franken genutzt wurde, muß Bedenken auslösen, da der Befund der Grabungen keinerlei Anhalt für diese Vermutung bietet, zudem wären die Franken beim Wiederaufbau wohl technisch überfordert gewesen. Dagegen bot der oben erwähnte Ostteil mit dem Saalbau auch von seiner Ausstattung her, die Mosaikfußböden waren wahrscheinlich noch weitgehend erhalten, weit bessere Möglichkeiten. Die Niederbauten um den großen Vorplatz südlich der Aula dürften weitgehend zerstört gewesen sein.

According to tradition, the Frankish *Gaugraf* (district leader) had his administrative seat in the area of the Roman complex. Without the roof and window glass, the large hall was no longer usable. Since its construction at the beginning of the 4th century, almost 350 years had past, so that signs of weathering were self-evident, discounting the damage inflicted during the events of the 5th century. The masonry itself, in some parts up to 9 ft/2.70 m thick, was almost indestructible. It can be assumed that the *Gaugraf* had his quarters in one of the side wings, with the sections located east of the hall being the best suited. The center of the facility was a smaller hall with an apse on the south end. To the north, behind the room, an entrance hall and a small courtyard were located, the latter probably accessible from smaller rooms to the north and east. The assumption that the great entrance hall of the Roman throne room was used by the Franks is questionable, as the excavation finds offer no support for this premise; furthermore, the Franks did not possess the technical know-how to rebuild the structure. In contrast, the above-mentioned east section with the smaller hall offered much better possibilities, also because of its appointments; the mosaic floors were presumably still preserved for the most part. The lower buildings around the large square south of the throne room were probably destroyed to a great extent.

Basilika mit Kurfürstlichem Palais. Pfeil: früher Bezirksregierung, heute Sitz der Aufsichts- und Dienstleistungsdirektion
"Basilika" with the Electoral Palace. Arrow: district administration

Lambert Dahm 95

Innenansicht des Saales östlich der Basilika um die Mitte des 7. Jhs.
Interior of the hall east of the Imperial throne room ("Basilika") around the middle of the 7ᵗʰ century

Die Reste dieser römischen Gebäude wurden bei der Umgestaltung des Palastinnenhofes 1985 entdeckt. Leider hat man beim Bau der Keller des kurfürstlichen Palastes größere Teile der Bauten abgegraben. Im Zentrum dieses Gebäudetraktes lag ein Saal mit einer Größe von 16,20 mal 10,75 m, wie bei Abb. 29 beschrieben, an den sich andere Räume anschlossen. Zwischen dem Saal und einem kleinen Innenhof lag eine Halle von über 24 m Länge und 8,50 m Breite, welche gleich dem Saal mit einem Mosaikfußboden ausgelegt war. Das Mosaik im Saal zeigte ein kleinteiliges, überwiegend ornamentales Dekor, nur an den Längswänden waren auf jeder Raumseite fünf Bilder angeordnet, von denen nur noch zwei fragmentarisch erhalten waren. Leider läßt diese perspektivische Ansicht nur eine Andeutung des Mosaiks zu. Die übrige Ausstattung des Raumes dürfte wohl im wesentlichen der großen Aula ähnlich gewesen sein und entsprach damit dem repräsentativen und künstlerischen Gesamtniveau der kaiserlichen Anlage. Es ist anzunehmen, daß die große Aula nur bei besonderen Anlässen benutzt wurde, während kleinere Empfänge usw. in den kleineren Sälen - ein weiterer lag auf der Westseite der Aula - stattfanden. Damit erklärt sich auch deren großartige Ausstattung. Diese Darstellung, sie zeigt einen angenommenen Empfang des Gaugrafen Mitte des 7. Jhs., unterstellt, daß der Saalbau die Krisenzeiten mit nur geringen Schäden überstanden hatte.

Innenansicht Basilika; die östliche Halle wird heute vom Innenhof verdeckt
Interior of the "Basilika"; today the east hall is covered by the inner courtyard

The remains of these Roman structures were discovered during the redesigning of the Palace courtyard in 1985. Regrettably, large sections of these buildings had been removed, including the foundations, when the cellar of the Electoral Palace was built. A hall measuring about 54 ft/16.2 m by 36 ft/10.75 m formed the center of this section, as described in illustration 29, connected with other rooms. Between the hall and a small courtyard stood another hall measuring 79 ft/24 m by 28 ft/8.5 m, which was laid out with a mosaic floor, as was the smaller hall. This mosaic consisted of small stones creating mostly ornamental decor. But a series of five pictures each, only two of which were preserved in fragments, ran in succession along the length of the hall on each side. Unfortunately, this perspective view permits only a suggestion of the mosaic. The rest of the room's appointments were presumably essentially similar to those of the large throne room and met the requirements of the ceremonial and artistic level of the Imperial complex. It may be assumed that the grand throne room was used for special occasions, whereas smaller receptions and the like took place in the smaller rooms - another was located on the west side of the throne room. That would explain the magnificent appointments. This reconstruction - it shows a suggested reception by the Gaugraf in the middle of the 7th century - postulates that the hall survived the crises of the 5ᵗʰ century with only little damage.

Die Basilika mit ihrer Umgebung nach der Mitte des 16. Jhs.
The "Basilika" (Imperial Throne Room) with its environs after the mid-16th century

Nach den Streitereien zwischen den Vögten und Ministerialengeschlechter einerseits und dem Erzbischof andererseits, der u.a. auch das Palatium betrafen, baute Erzbischof Johann I. (1189-1212) die Basilika fast festungsähnlich mit Zinnen bewehrt zu einer Burg aus.

Als wichtige Vorlage für diese Rekonstruktion diente eine Zeichnung bei Alexander Wiltheim von ca. 1636. Die Mauerkronen der Apsis wie auch die des Saales waren mit Zinnen ausgebaut, hinter denen wahrscheinlich auch ein Wehrgang lag. Das Dach konnte von den vier Türmchen aus erreicht werden. Die großen römischen Fenster waren vermauert und durch kleine ersetzt. Vor dem Nordwestturm der Basilika erhob sich die Laurentiuskirche, deren Anfänge in das 8. Jh. zurückreichen. Die Kirche veränderte im Laufe der Zeit ihr Aussehen, so zum Beispiel zu Beginn des 16. Jhs., als die Bauteile an der Nordseite angefügt wurden. Das Areal nördlich der Kirche und der Basilikaapsis ist noch von Wohnbauten belegt, die durch Kurfürst Johann VII. von Schönenberg (1581-1599) angekauft und abgebrochen wurden. Die Mauer im Bildvordergrund wird neuerlich mit der Ludolfschen Mauer (Schutzmauer der Domfreiheit) in Verbindung gebracht. Im Hintergrund sind die Ruinen der Kaiserthermen zu sehen. In deren Palaestra stand die alte Gervasiuskirche. Dahinter erkennt man noch die mittelalterliche Stadtmauer.

After the conflicts between the bailiffs and government officers on the one side and the archbishop on the other, conflicts concerning, among other things, the *palatium*, Archbishop John 1 (1189-1212) converted the "Basilika" to an almost fortress-like castle armed with battlements.

A drawing by Alexander Wiltheim from around 1636 served as an important model for this reconstruction. The top of the apse wall as well as that of the hall were equipped with battlements, behind which presumably a sentry walk was located. The roof could be reached from the four turrets. The large Roman windows were replaced by smaller ones. The Church of St. Lawrence, whose origins date to the 8th century, rose next to the northwest tower of the "Basilika." The church altered its appearance in the course of the centuries, for example, at the beginning of the 16th century, when the sections on the north side were added. The area north of the church and the "Basilika" apse is still occupied by houses which were bought by Elector John VII of Schonenberg (1581-1599) and torn down. The wall in the picture foreground has recently been associated with Ludolf's wall (protective wall for the Cathedral city). In the background, the ruins of the Imperial Baths are visible. To the right of the ruins, on the old sports grounds, is St. Gervasius's church. And behind that is the medieval city wall.

Die Umgebung der Basilika hat sich mit dem Anbau des Palais völlig verändert.
The "Basilika" environs was completely altered when the Palace was adjoined to it.

Der Schatten der Basilika markiert die Lage der Laurentiuskirche
The shadow of the "Basilika" marks the position of St. Lawrence's.

Der Kurfürstliche Palast um 1750
The Electoral Palace around 1750

Der Standpunkt des Betrachters bei dieser Rekonstruktion liegt etwa an der Straßenecke "An der Meerkatz" und Konstantinplatz mit Blick auf die Apsis der umgebauten Basilika. Mit der alten Laurentiuskirche bildet die Baugruppe ein für uns heute völlig ungewohntes Bild. Von der Laurentiuskirche, deren Anfänge bis in merowingische Zeit zurückgehen, gibt es kaum Abbildungen. Sie war in Ost-Westrichtung unmittelbar an die Basilika angebaut und hatte, wie die Baugliederung auch zeigt, verschiedene Phasen der Erweiterung und Umgestaltung erfahren, die umfassendste im Jahre 1515. 1803 wurde sie, wie viele andere Kirchen und Klöster, abgebrochen. Als wichtige Stütze für ihre Rekonstruktion diente die bei Abb. 31 erwähnte Zeichnung von Alexander Wiltheim.

1750 stand der Renaissancepalast bereits über 100 Jahre. Der Neubau des barocken Südflügels (zum heutigen Palastgarten stehend) sollte bald unter Kurfürst Johann von Walderdorff (1756-1768) erfolgen. Am rechten Bildrand ist noch ein Teil der um 1745 erbauten Orangerie zu erkennen.

An die Apsis der Basilika schloß sich bis zur Basilikawiederherstellung (zwischen 1848 und 1856), der Portalflügel mit dem Petrustor des kurfürstlichen Palastes an. Das großartige Portal war der Haupteingang zum Palast und die Einfahrt zu den Höfen der Palastanlage. Der sich nach Osten anschließende Rote Turm (Archivgebäude der kurfürstlichen Administration) ist hier nicht mehr erfaßt.

In this reconstruction, the observer's position lies near the corner of "An der Meerkatz" and Constantine Square, with a view toward the apse of the converted "Basilika." With old St. Lawrence's, the complex takes on a completely unaccustomed appearance for us today. Hardly any depictions of St. Lawrence's exist, a church dating back to the Merovingian period. It was built onto the "Basilika" in an east-west direction and underwent, as the arrangement of the structure shows, various phases of extension and remodeling, the most comprehensive in 1515. In 1803, it was torn down, as were many other churches, monasteries, and convents. As mentioned in the text for picture 31, the same drawing by Alexander Wiltheim served as model for its reconstruction.

In 1750, the Renaissance palace had already stood over 100 years. The new structure of the baroque south wing (facing the present-day Palace Garden) under Elector John Phillip of Walderdorff (1756-1768) would soon follow. On the right side of the picture, a part of the orangery from around 1745 is visible.

The portal wing with St. Peter's Gate to the Electoral Palace adjoined the "Basilika" apse until the restoration of the "Basilika" (between 1848 and 1856). The magnificent portal was the main entrance to the palace and the drive into the courtyards of the palace complex. The adjacent Red Tower to the north (archives building of the Electoral administration) is not in the picture.

Blick auf das Petersburgportal des 17. Jhs. Pfeil links: der Rote Turm von 1647
View of the St. Peterburg Portal from the 17th century. Arrow left: the Red Tower from 1647

Lambert Dahm 99

Der Kurfürstliche Palast um 1780
The Electoral Palace around 1780

Die Nachrichten über die Bautätigkeit der frühen Palastanlage sind sehr spärlich und werden erst vom 16. Jh. an überschaubarer. Sie begannen mit dem Ankauf und Abriß der Wohnanlagen nördlich von Basilikaapsis und Laurentiuskirche. Unter Kurfürst Lothar von Metternich (1599-1623) wurden im Zusammenhang mit dem Neubau des Palatiums die Ostwand und der größte Teil der Südwand der Basilika (Kaiseraula) abgebrochen. Wie das Bild zeigt, wird die Basilika niedriger, das Mauerwerk etwa oberhalb der Kämpferhöhe der Pfeilerbögen wurde abgetragen. Die Basilikawestseite wurde zum Westflügel der Renaissanceanlage, zu der auch der "Rote Turm", ein Kanzlei- und Archivgebäude (an der Nordwestecke des Bereiches), gehörte. Deutlich sind der Renaissanceinnenhof sowie die dahinterliegenden Gebäude mit dem Marstall zu erkennen. Repräsentativster Teil des Palatiums ist der 1761 vollendete, im Rokokostil erbaute Südflügel. An seiner Südwestecke stand die um 1745 erbaute und 1802 abgebrochene Orangerie. Vor dem Südflügel lag der Palastgarten, dessen Entwurf der Hofarchitekten Johannes Seiz fertigte, der Garten wurde aber wahrscheinlich nicht vollendet. An der Nordwestecke der Basilika ist die Laurentiuskirche zu sehen, während man in der unteren linken Bildecke die Weberbach erkennen kann. Diagonal dazu, in der oberen rechten Bildecke, sieht man die Mustorstraße und das Mustor, das nach Osten führende Stadttor.

Das kurfürstliche Palais mit der Basilika. Blaues Dach: Hauptgebäude der Kreisverwaltung Trier-Saarburg
The Electoral Palace with the "Basilika." Blue roof: main building of the Trier-Saarburg County Administration

Information about the building activity concerning the early palace complex is very limited and did not become clear until the 16th century. These activities began with the purchase and demolition of the houses north of the "Basilika" apse and St. Lawrence's. As a part of the new construction of the *palatium*, Elector Lothar of Metternich (1599-1623) had the east wall and the major portion of the south wall of the "Basilika" (Imperial throne room) torn down. As the picture shows, the height of the "Basilika" was reduced: the upper portion of the long wall was removed down to the level just above where the arches of the original windows began. The west side of the "Basilika" became the west wing of the Renaissance complex, which included the "Red Tower," a chancellery and archives building (at the northwest corner of the complex). Clearly visible are the Renaissance inner courtyard and the buildings behind with the stables. The most splendid part of the palace is the south wing, completed in 1761 in rococo style. The orangery, built around 1745 and demolished in 1802, stood at the southwest corner of the rococo wing. The Palace Garden was designed by court architect John Seiz to spread out in front of the south wing; it was probably not finished. St. Lawrence's is visible at the northwest corner of the "Basilika"; the street of the Weavers' Brook is visible in the lower left corner. Diagonally opposite, in the upper right corner, Mustorstrasse and the Mustor gate lead out of the city to the east.

Lambert Dening

Der Hauptmarkt zu Beginn des 12. Jhs.
The present-day Main Market at the beginning of the 12th century

Der kurz nach der Mitte des 10. Jhs. von Erzbischof Heinrich I. (956-964) gestiftete Markt lag unmittelbar vor der Domstadt, welche nach der Zerstörung der Stadt durch die Normannen 882 zur Keimzelle des neuen, mittelalterlichen Trier wurde. Der neue Markt wurde schon bald zum neuen Zentrum der Stadt, das er bis in unsere Tage geblieben ist. Erzbischof Heinrich I. ließ im Jahre 958 auch das Marktkreuz errichten. In der linken Bildhälfte erkennt man den sogenannten Turm Jerusalem, einen Wohnturm, wie sie im 11. Jh. von adeligen Familien erbaut wurden. Er ist im unteren Teil bis heute erhalten und in den Baukomplex des Palais Walderdorff integriert. Gut erkennbar ist auch die um das Jahr 1000 unter Erzbischof Ludolf (994-1008) errichtete Schutzmauer um die Domimmunität, die sogenannte Ludolfsche Mauer, mit dem Tor zum Markt hin, das in der heutigen Sternstraße stand. Der Name Sternstraße geht auf die mittelalterliche Torbezeichnung "sub posterna", was "unterm Bogen" bedeutete, zurück. Im Verlauf des 11. Jhs. wurden erste Häuser an die Schutzmauer angebaut, die noch einfacher Art waren. Sie waren mit ziemlicher Sicherheit eingeschossig und nicht vergleichbar mit den Wohnbauten des 13. und 14. Jahrhunderts. Der Dom im Hintergrund hatte seine neue Westfassade erst wenige Jahrzehnte zuvor unter Erzbischof Poppo (1016-1047) erhalten. Das Bild versucht, etwas von der Aufbruchstimmung des frühen 12. Jhs., etwa um das Jahr 1120, zu vermitteln.

The market founded shortly after the mid-10th century by Archbishop Henry I (956-964) is located directly outside the Cathedral city; it became the nucleus of medieval Trier after the destruction of the city by the Vikings in 882. This newly founded market would soon become the center of the city, which it has remained to the present-day. Archbishop Henry I also had the market cross erected in 958.
Jerusalem Tower is visible on the left side of the picture, a dwelling tower such as those built by families of the nobility in the 11th century. The lower section has been preserved up to the present and is integrated into the Walderdorff Palace complex. Also visible is the protective wall surrounding the Cathedral city, built under Archbishop Ludolf (994-1008) around 1000, with its gate to the market which stood in present-day Sternstrasse. The name Sternstrasse originates in the medieval name for the gate, "Posterna," here meaning "archway." In the course of the 11th century, a few houses, still very plain, were built against the exterior of the wall. They were most certainly of only one story and not comparable to the dwellings of the 13th and 14th centuries. The Cathedral in the background had had its new west section for only a few decades, built under Archbishop Poppo (1016-1047). The picture attempts to impart something of the spirit of optimism of the early 12th century, around 1120.

Blick über den Hauptmarkt auf den Domfreihof mit Dom und Liebfrauen. Pfeil: Palais Walderdorff mit Turm Jerusalem (Standesamt)
View across Main Market toward Cathedral Square, Cathedral and Our Lady's. Arrow: Walderdorff Palace with Jerusalem Tower (registrar's office)

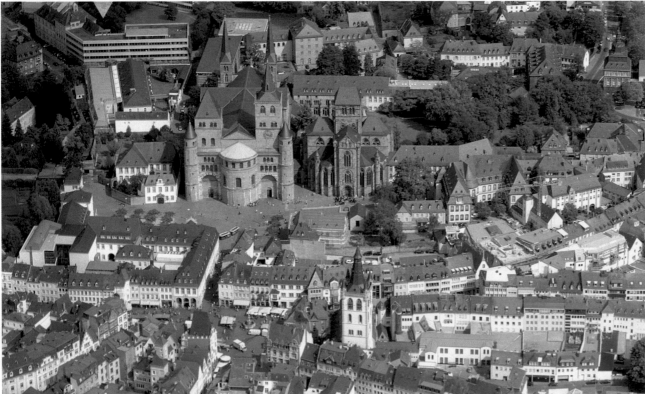

Die Ostseite des Hauptmarktes um 1490
The east side of the Main Market around 1490

Der Blick richtet sich etwa, wie auch bei Abb. 34, von der Steipe gegen Osten in Richtung Dom. An der linken Bildseite erkennt man den Wohnturm Jerusalem aus dem 11. Jahrhundert. Vergleicht man die beiden Bilder, so wird der Wandel deutlich, den der Hauptmarkt in den mehr als dreieinhalb Jahrhunderten erlebt hat. An Stelle des Tores zur Domstadt in der Sternstraße zeigt nunmehr ein Bogen den Beginn der Domimmunität an. Dieser Bogen ist auf einer Zeichnung von Gerhard Nauen aus dem Jahre 1571 erhalten. Eine andere Zeichnung des Gerhard Nauen aus dem Jahre 1558 zeigt die Nordostecke des Hauptmarktes mit dem sogenannten Fischbach. Dieser Teil des Hauptmarktes, der sogenannte Fischmarkt, war für die Fischverkäufer reserviert,

die hier ihre Ware anboten. Sie hielten ihre Fische zum Teil im unmittelbar vorbeifließenden Stadtbach (hier perspektivisch bedingt nur als schmaler Streifen zu sehen) frisch. Nauens Zeichnung (detailgenau mit der Darstellung von Fischbehältern) liegt zwar 70 Jahre später als der gewählte Zeitpunkt der Rekonstruktion, hier darf man wohl davon ausgehen, daß sich in dieser relativ kurzen Zeit die bauliche Situation nicht wesentlich geändert hat. Auch an diesem Teil des Marktes blieb die alte Parzellierung bis heute fast unverändert, sieht man von dem Vorsprung des Vorgängerbauwerkes des Palais Walderdorff einmal ab.

Blick über den Hauptmarkt von Westen auf Dom und Liebfrauen. Pfeil Mitte: Marktkreuz. Pfeil rechts: Petrusbrunnen
View across Main Market from the west toward the Cathedral and Our Lady. Middle arrow: Market Cross. Arrow right: St. Peter's Fountain

As in illustration 34, the view is directed from the Steipe toward the east in the direction of the Cathedral. Jerusalem Tower from the 11th century is visible on the left side. In a comparison of the two pictures, the transformation which the Main Market had experienced in the more than three-and-a-half centuries becomes obvious. Instead of the gate to the Cathedral city in Sternstrasse, an arch now shows the entrance to the enclosure. This arch is preserved on a drawing by Gerhard Nauen from 1571. Another Nauen drawing from 1558 shows the northeast corner of the Main Market with the so-called Fish Brook. This part of the market, called Fish Market, was reserved for the fish sellers who offered their catch here. Some of them kept their fish fresh in the brook flowing directly across the market (visible only as a narrow strip in this perspective). Although Nauen's drawing (with exact details of the fish containers) was done 70 years later than the time chosen for the reconstruction, it may be assumed that the site had not been essentially altered in this relative short time. And the old building sites have remained almost unchanged up to the present, except for the projection of the predecessor of the Walderdorff Palace

Süd- und Westseite des Hauptmarktes um 1490
South and west side of the Main Market around 1490

Bei diesem Bild ist der Blick aus der Sternstraße auf die Südwestecke des Hauptmarktes und die Steipe gerichtet. Zu diesem Zeitpunkt ist die dargestellte Steipe (1483) noch kein Jahrzehnt vollendet, der Turm der Marktkirche St. Gangolf hat noch nicht die beiden von Adelheid von Besselich gestifteten oberen Stockwerke, die erst 1507 aufgesetzt wurden. Dadurch erscheint der Turm uns heute ungewohnt und fremd. In der vorderen Fleischstraße fehlt noch das um 1557 erbaute Zunfthaus der Schiffer (siehe Abb. 39). Da sich die Parzellierung auch in diesem Teil des Hauptmarktes seit damals nicht wesentlich geändert hat, dürfte die Rekonstruktion der damaligen Bebauung recht nahe kommen.

Der Marktplatz hatte zu dieser Zeit noch keinen Brunnen. Der erste Brunnen, dessen Fassung ebenfalls eine Stiftung der Adelheid von Besselich war, wurde erst 1496 errichtet (siehe hierzu Abb. 37-39). Ihm folgte dann etwa 100 Jahre später (1595 vollendet) der von Erzbischof Johann VII. (1581-1599) gestiftete Brunnen von H. R. Hoffmann. In der linken unteren Bildecke sind noch die Abdeckplatten des Stadtbaches zu erkennen, der aus der Sternstraße kommend vorbei am Fischmarkt durch die Simeonstraße in Richtung Simeonstift und von dort zur Mosel floß. Der Markt war sicher weit belebter als hier dargestellt, zugunsten der Architektur wurde auf weitergehende Ausdeutung des Marktgeschehens verzichtet.

In this picture, the view is directed from Sternstrasse to the southwest corner of the Main Market and the Steipe. At this time (1483), the Steipe had been finished for less than ten years; the tower on the market church, St. Gangolf's, did not yet have the two upper stories which were built in 1507 as a bequest by Adelheid of Besselich. Thus the tower appears odd and unfamiliar. The guild house of the river boatmen (1557, see illustration 39) had also not yet been built at the beginning of Fleischstrasse. As the building sites on this section of the Main Market have also hardly been altered since that time, the reconstruction of the site may be considered close to reality.

At this time the market place has no fountain or well. The first fountain for drinking water, also a bequest by Adelheid of Besselich, was constructed in 1496 (see illustrations 37-39). About 100 years later (completed in 1595), Archbishop John VII (1581-1599) donated a fountain designed by H. R. Hoffmann. The tiles covering the city brook are visible in the lower left corner of the picture; the brook flowed from Sternstrasse past the fish market through Simeonstrasse in the direction of Simeon's College and from there to the Moselle. The market was certainly busier than pictured here, but the reconstruction dispenses with more detailed market activity in favor of depicting the architecture.

Hauptmarkt von Nordosten. Pfeil links: St. Gangolf. Pfeil Mitte: Steipe
Main Market from the northeast. Arrow left: St. Gangolf's. Arrow middle: Steipe

Marktkreuz von 958 mit dem Lamm Gottes
Market Cross from 958 with the Lamb of God

Lambert Dahm 1996

Der gotische Marktbrunnen am Hauptmarkt um 1575

The Gothic fountain on Main Market around 1575

Um 1575 standen im Bereich des Hauptmarktes nicht weniger als drei Brunnen. Die Nachricht über deren Existenz wird einem Bericht des kaiserlichen Kommissars German Erndlin aus dem Jahre 1571 verdankt.

Danach stand neben dem Vorgänger des heutigen Marktbrunnens ein weiterer in der Grabenstraße und ein dritter im Bereich der Einmündung Dietrichstraße/Fleischstraße. Der im Jahre 1496 erbaute gotische Brunnen wurde durch die nach 1494 erbaute neue Wasserleitung gespeist, deren Quellen in der Nähe von Heiligkreuz lagen. Auf der bei Abb. 35 erwähnten Zeichnung Nauens von 1571 ist u.a. auch dieser Brunnen dargestellt, allerdings nur in minimaler Größe. Es ist die einzige Darstellung des Brunnens überhaupt. Nach dieser Zeichnung handelte es sich um einen gotischen Stockbrunnen mit hexagonalem Grundriß. Erndlin beschreibt ihn als einen großen, hohen Brunnen, der einen steinernen Brunnentrog mit großem Fassungsvermögen hatte. Aus seiner Mitte erhob sich eine hohe Steinsäule mit sechs Wasserrohren. Über diesen Wasserrohren war die Säule mit gotischer Spitzgiebelornamentik geziert, auf deren höherer mittlerer Spitze eine steinerne vergoldete Petrusfigur stand. Diese Beschreibung deckt sich mit der Skizze Nauens. Der wohl aus zu weichem Steinmaterial gefertigte Brunnen wurde im April 1595 abgebrochen und drei Monaten später durch den Renaissancebrunnen ersetzt, der heute noch den Hauptmarkt ziert.

Around 1575, no fewer than three sources of drinking water stood on the site around the Main Market. The information about their existence is contained in a report by the Imperial Commissioner German Erndlin from 1571.

According to the report, besides the predecessor to the present-day market fountain, a further source of water was located in Grabenstrasse and a third in the area of the intersection of Dietrichstrasse and Fleischstrasse. The Gothic fountain built in 1496 was fed by the new water conduit assembled after 1494, with its source near Holy Cross Hill. This fountain is also sketched in the Nauen drawing from 1571 mentioned in the text to illustration 35, but only in very small size. It is the only depiction of the fountain that exists. According to this drawing, it was a Gothic fountain with a hexagonal basin. Erndlin describes it as a large, tall fountain with a stone basin of considerable capacity. From its center rose a tall stone column with six water spouts. Above the water spouts, the column was ornamented with pointed Gothic spires; the taller central spire was crowned by a gilded stone statue of St. Peter. This description matches the fountain in Nauen's sketch. The fountain was torn down in April 1595, probably because the stone was too soft, and replaced three months later by the Renaissance fountain still gracing the Main Market today.

Blick auf den Petrusbrunnen gegenüber der Steipe
View toward St. Peter's Fountain across from the Steipe

Detail Petrusbrunnen: Petrus, der Stadtpatron
Detail St. Peter's Fountain: St. Peter, city's patron saint

Der Brunnen in der Grabenstraße
The well in Grabenstrasse

Auch die Kenntnisse über diesen zweiten Brunnen, unweit vom Hauptmarkt in der Grabenstraße, werden dem Bericht des Kommissars Erndlin verdankt. Danach befand sich der Brunnen etwa im unteren Drittel der Grabenstraße zur Palaststraße und Brotstraße hin. Leider steht die Beschreibungen des Brunnens im Widerspruch zu der Skizze von Nauen. Da keine weiteren Unterlagen zur Verfügung stehen, muß die Logik entscheiden. Dabei erscheint der Bericht Erndlins glaubwürdiger, da er die

Standorte, die Umgebung und die Brunnen selbst eingehend beschreibt. Auf der Skizze Nauens fehlt der in der Grabenstraße beschriebene Brunnen, an seiner Stelle steht der von Erndlin in der Fleischstraße beschriebene Brunnen, dessen Standort bei Nauen unbesetzt ist.

Im Gegensatz zum Marktbrunnen wurde dieser Brunnen durch Grundwasser gespeist. Es war wohl ein relativ einfacher Schöpfbrunnen, der nach Erndlin aus gehauenen Quadersteinen gemauert war. Nach Norden und Süden hin war er seitlich geschlossen, die beiden übrigen Seiten standen offen. Der obere Teil des Brunnens war nach oben spitz gewölbt und mit einer Petrusfigur bekrönt, die in Richtung Hauptmarkt schaute. Der Brunnen war nicht farbig gefaßt und nach einer Gewölbeinschrift im Jahre 1563 errichtet worden. Die Rekonstruktion zeigt den Brunnen etwa vom Zugang zur Palaststraße her gesehen. Im gleichen Straßenteil soll auch der Pranger gestanden haben.

Die Grabenstraße vor St. Gangolf. Pfeil oben: Frankenturm. Pfeil unten: der Pranger
Grabenstrasse at St. Gangolf's. Arrow above: Franco's Tower. Arrow below: the pillory

The knowledge of the second water source, a well not far from the Main Market in Grabenstrasse, is also owing to Commissioner Erndlin's report. This report states that the well house stood in the lower third of Grabenstrasse toward Palaststrasse and Brotstrasse. Unfortunately, the description of the well house contradicts Nauen's sketch. As no other records exist, logic must decide. Erndlin's reports seems to be the more credible, as he describes in detail the position, the surroundings, and the well house itself. Nauen's drawing does not show the well described in Grabenstrasse; the well reported in Fleischstrasse stands in its place. Nauen's drawing shows no well at all in the position in Fleischstrasse.

In contrast to the market fountain, this well's source was, of course, ground water. It was likely a relatively simple form, with the wellhead protected by a stone base as described by Erndlin. Above this base, it was closed on the north and south sides and open on the two other sides. The upper section of the well house was vaulted to a point, crowned by a statue of St. Peter facing toward the Main Market. According to an inscription on the vaulted top, the well house was erected in 1563; the stone structure was left in the natural state. The reconstruction shows the well from the entrance to Palaststrasse. The pillory is said to have stood in this same section of the street.

Lambert Dahm 98

Der dritte Brunnen an der Ecke Fleischstraße/Dietrichstraße

The third water source at the corner of Fleischstrasse and Dietrichstrasse

Wie bei Abb. 38 bemerkt, beschreibt Erndlin an dieser Stelle einen Brunnen, der bei Nauen fehlt. Dieser war wohl der einfachste der drei Brunnen. Nach dem Bericht hatte er einen kreisförmigen Grundriß. Nach der Zeichnung Nauens, er verlegte diesen Brunnen in die Grabenstraße, erhob sich über einem kreisrunden Sockelkranz die Brunnenwandung, auf der wiederum ein Ringgesims lag. Darauf stand nach Erndlin

Unter der Steipefigur des Jakobus des Älteren befindet sich hochkant die Trierische Elle (56,5 cm)
The Trier ell (22.25 in/56.5 cm) is mounted below the Steipe statue of St. James the Elder

ein hölzernes Häuschen mit einer Tür und einem spitzen Schieferdächlein. An dessen Spitze war eine eiserne Fahne angebracht, auf deren rotem Grund eine goldene Petrusfigur aufgemalt war. Bei Nauen ruhte das Dach des Brunnens auf sechs Stützen, wodurch der gesamte Brunnenaufbau oberhalb des Ringgesimses sechseckig wurde. Bei ihm ist nichts von einem Häuslein mit Tür zu erkennen, obwohl die Konstruktion durchaus glaubhaft erscheint.

Das Türlein, das Erndlin erwähnt, war vielleicht nur die Öffnung zum Wasserschöpfen. Mit einem wie auf der Rekonstruktion angenommenen Holzaufbau konnte man den Brunnentrog schützen, um das häufig beklagte Tränken der Tiere und die damit verbundene Verschmutzung des Wassers zu unterbinden. Der Brunnen wurde ebenfalls mit Grundwasser gespeist. Die Rekonstruktion gibt ein Bild des Brunnens wieder, das dem Original sehr nahe kommen dürfte. Bei dem großen Giebelhaus hinter dem Brunnen handelt es sich um das ehemalige Zunfthaus der Schiffer und Schiffbauer, das 1557 erbaut wurde.

As noted in illustration 38, Erndlin describes a well for this position that is lacking in the Nauen drawing. The superstructure was surely the plainest setting of the three water sources. According to the report, the well house had a circular stone base. According to the Nauen drawing - he placed it in Grabenstrasse - a circular stone base rose above ground level, topped by a projecting stone ring, on which stood, according to Erndlin, a wooden housing with a door and a pointed slate-covered roof. An iron flag with a golden figure of St. Peter painted on a red background was mounted at the top. In the Nauen drawing, the well house roof rested on six supports, with the entire well house above the hexagonal stone ring. The drawing shows no well house with a door, although the construction appears completely credible.

The small door that Erndlin mentions was perhaps only the opening to the well house. The trough inside the well house could be protected by the wooden house postulated in the reconstruction, in order to prevent animals from drinking from the trough, an often lamented practice that led to water contamination. The water source was ground water here as well. The reconstruction reflects a picture of the well believably close to the original. The large house with the three gable stories behind the well was the former guild house of the river boatmen and shipbuilders, built in 1557.

Blick von der Steipe auf Dom und Liebfrauen zu Beginn des 17. Jhs.

View from the Steipe toward the Cathedral and Our Lady at the beginning of the 17th century

Dieser Blick aus einem Dachgeschoßfenster des Steipeninnenhofes ist für den Betrachters ungewohnt, aber dafür um so interessanter. Das Bild zeigt die Liebfrauenkirche im frühen 17. Jh. noch mit ihrem alles überragenden Turmhelm, wie er auch von alten Stichen bekannt ist. Der Turm in dieser Form stammte aus dem 15. Jahrhundert, er wurde bis 1447 erneuert, nachdem er 1423 durch einen Blitzschlag in Brand geraten und völlig zerstört worden war. Dieser erneuerte Turmhelm wurde im Juli 1631 bei einem schweren Sturm zerstört. Danach erhielt der Turm einen stumpfen Helm etwa in seiner heutigen Form. Der Dom-Südwestturm wurde unter Erzbischof Richard von Greiffenklau (1511-1531) erhöht. Blickfang im Vordergrund ist die Steipe, welche 1483 als Fest- und Trinkhaus des Stadtrates fertiggestellt wurde. Hier ist die Steipe noch unberührt und frei von späteren Veränderungen. Durch die Zerstörung im Krieg und den erfolgten Wiederaufbau ging viel von der alten Romantik verloren. Gleich neben der Steipe stand zu dieser Zeit (Anfang des 17. Jhs.) noch der gotische Vorgängerbau des sogenannten Roten Hauses, das erst 1684 erbaut wurde und seinen Namen dem ursprünglich roten Anstrich verdankt. An seiner Fassade stand der bekannte Spruch „Eher als Rom stand Trier 1300 Jahre ...", der ursprünglichen an der alten Steipe stand.

Der Treppenturm im Vordergrund links stammt aus dem Jahre 1559 und ist auch heute ein Teil des immer noch schönen Steipeninnenhofes.

This view from a dormer window in the Steipe inner courtyard is an unusual one for the observer and thus all the more interesting. The picture shows Our Lady's Church in the early 17th century when it still had its helm roof towering over all else, as is known from old engravings. The tower in this form dates from the 15th century; it was renewed in 1447 after it had been struck by lightning in 1423 and was destroyed by fire. This rebuilt helm tower was then devastated by a severe storm in July 1631. Afterwards, the tower was given a squat roof resembling its present form. The southwest tower of the Cathedral was raised under Archbishop Richard of Greiffenklau (1511-1531). The picture focuses on the Steipe in the foreground, which was finished in 1483 as a festival and drinking hall for the city council. Here the Steipe is shown still untouched and free of later alterations. Much of the old romantic atmosphere of the structure was lost through the bombing in World War II and the subsequent rebuilding. At this time (beginning of the 17th century), the Gothic predecessor of the so-called Red House stood directly next to the Steipe. This Red House was not built until 1684 and owes it name to its originally red façade, on which could be read the well-known pronouncement "Trier stood 1300 years before Rome ...," initially to be found on the old Steipe.

The stair tower in the left foreground dates from 1559 and is still a part of the lovely Steipe inner courtyard.

Blick über den Steipeinnenhof auf den Dom
View across the Steipe courtyard toward the Cathedral

Detail der Steipefassade: Wasserspeier und Engel
Detail of the Steipe façade: gargoyle and angel

Lambert Dahm 99

Der sogenannte Frankenturm
Franco's Tower

Durch seinen Namen wird der Turm häufig mit den Franken in Verbindung gebracht. Der Name geht aber auf seinen Besitzer im 14. Jh., Franco von Senheim, zurück. Erbaut wurde der Frankenturm im 11. Jh. aus überwiegend antikem Steinmaterial. Ein von einer antiken Inschrift stammender Rest wurde zum Beispiel über der Eingangstür als Türsturz eingebaut. Das Bauwerk war einer der Wohn- und Wehrtürme in der Stadt, wie sie von Angehörigen der städtischen Führungsschicht, hauptsächlich Adelsgeschlechtern, erbaut wurden und nicht zuletzt auch der Repräsentation seiner Besitzer dienten. Diese Türme, deren Eingänge vom Straßenniveau unerreichbar im ersten Obergeschoß lagen, waren nur über einen nach außen liegenden leiterartigen, heraufziehbaren Aufgang zugänglich. Die Fenster waren klein gehalten und wirkten fast wie Schießscharten. Eine Ausnahme bildeten nur das hier zur Straße liegende große Doppelfenster des Wohnraumes, das im romanischen Stil gestaltet ist. Das Dach lag verborgen hinter dem zinnenbestückten oberen Geschoß. Auf die Ähnlichkeit mit dem Turm Jerusalem im Bereich des heutigen Palais Walderdorff (Abb. 34 und 35) wurde bereits hingewiesen. Diese Türme, welche meist Teil größerer Hofanlagen waren, verloren nach dem endgültigen Ausbau der Stadtmauer im 13. Jh. weitgehend ihre Bedeutung als Wehranlagen. Das Bild versucht, eine Situation wiederzugeben, wie sie sich um 1250 in der heutigen Dietrichstraße dargeboten haben könnte.

Because of its German name (Frankenturm), the tower is frequently associated with the Germanic Franks. But the name refers to its owner in the 14th century, Franco of Senheim. The dwelling tower was erected in the 11th century of mostly ancient Roman stone material. For example, a fragment of an ancient inscription stone was built into the entry as the door lintel. The structure was a dwelling and defensive tower inside the city, like those built by members of the city's ruling class, mainly clans of the nobility, and used by their owners also for ceremonial duties. These towers, whose entries were located in the upper story and thus inaccessible from street level, were reached by way of a retractable ladder-like stairs located on the exterior. The windows were small and appeared almost like loop windows on fortifications. The large Romanesque double living room window facing the street represents the exception. The roof lay hidden behind the battlements on the topmost story. The similarity to Jerusalem Tower near the present-day Walderdorff Palace (illustrations 34 and 35) has already been mentioned. These towers, which generally were part of larger estates, lost their significance as defensive structures after the medieval city wall was finally completed in the 13th century. The picture attempts to render a state as it might have appeared in Dietrichstrasse around 1250.

Blick auf den heute von allen Seiten eingeengten Frankenturm
View toward Franco's Tower, closed in on all sides today

Frankenturm mit Doppelfenster über modernem Tor
Franco's Tower with double window above modern door

Lambert Dahm 199?

Das alte Trierer Kauf- und Rathaus am Kornmarkt um 1575
The old Trier store and city hall at the Grain Market around 1575

Dieses alte Kauf- und Rathaus der Stadt, Ecke Kornmarkt und Fleischstraße gelegen, fand weit weniger Aufmerksamkeit als die Steipe am Hauptmarkt. Es wurde wohl durch die Verbindung mit dem Handel, dessen Lagerplätze fast bis an das Gebäude reichten, nicht als gleich repräsentativ empfunden wie die Steipe am Hauptmarkt. Erbaut wurde das Rathaus um die Mitte des 15. Jhs. Laut einer Steuerliste aus dem Jahre 1364 hatte am Kornmarkt bereits an gleicher Stelle ein Rathaus gestanden, das wahrscheinlich im 13. Jh. erbaut worden war. Das Bauwerk des 15. Jhs. hatte im Erdgeschoß eine große offene Halle, ähnlich der Steipe, in welcher fremde Kaufleute die Möglichkeit hatten, ihrer Stapelpflicht (Warenangebot) nachzukommen. Darüber lag ein Festsaal, in welchem u.a. 1473 die Eröffnung der Trierer Universität gefeiert wurde. Der Baukomplex wurde durch verschiedene tiefgreifende Baumaßnahmen stark verändert, ehe er nach schweren Bombenschäden 1944 weitgehend zerstört und 1952 abgebrochen wurde. Im 18. Jh. wurde die verkommene Bauanlage samt Lagerplatz umgestaltet. 1750-1751 wurde der Georgsbrunnen erbaut, und 13 Jahre später wurde die Verbindung zwischen Fleischstraße und Brotstraße durch den Bau der heutigen Johann-Philipp-Straße geschaffen. Die umfassendste Veränderung erfuhr das Bauwerk im Jahre 1856, als östlich daneben ein neues Rathaus erbaut wurde. Das Kaufhaus erhielt eine fast neue Fassade, welche von der alten Außenhaut wahrscheinlich nur geringe Reste übrig ließ.

This old store and city hall, located at the corner of Fleischstrasse and the Grain Market, did not attract as much attention as the Steipe on the Main Market. Presumably because of its association with trade - its stacking area reached almost to the building itself - it was not considered as splendid as the Steipe. The city hall was erected around the mid-15th century. According to a tax list from 1364, the Grain Market already had a city hall in the same location, probably constructed in the 13th century. The building of the 15th century had a large open hall on the ground floor, similar to the one in the Steipe, where out-of-town merchants had the possibility of fulfilling their obligation to sell their wares. In the next story was a hall for festivities, where, among other events, the opening of the Trier University was celebrated in 1473. The complex was greatly transformed by various drastic alterations before it was finally torn down in 1952 after it had been virtually destroyed by the massive bombing in 1944. In the 18th century, the dilapidated facility, including the stacking area, was remodeled. In 1750-1751, St. George's fountain was erected, and the link between Fleischstrasse and Brotstrasse was created 13 years later by the construction of the present-day Johann-Philipp-Strasse. The hall experienced its most comprehensive alteration in 1856, when a new city hall was built to the east of it. The store received an almost new façade, which probably retained only a few remains of the old exterior.

Blick auf den Kornmart. Pfeil: Lage des früheren Rathauses links von der großen Zeder
View toward the Grain Market. Arrow: position of the former city hall to the left of the large cedar tree

Der Georgsbrunnen für Kurfürst Franz Georg von Schönborn
St. George's Fountain for Elector Francis George of Schönborn

Die Moselbrücke gegen Ende des 14. Jhs.
The Moselle bridge toward the end of the 14th century

Die Pfeiler dieser Brücke sind römischen Ursprungs und gehören zu der um die Mitte des 2. Jhs. erbauten sogenannten Römerbrücke. Sie diente etwa 1200 Jahre wohl als einziger überlebender fester Flußübergang der Mosel zwischen Metz und Koblenz. Ihre Pfeiler trugen bis heute alle späteren Brücken. Die römischen Brücken waren Holzkonstruktionen, welche auf den steinernen Pfeilern auflagen. Die erste gewölbte Steinbrücke wurde unter Erzbischof Balduin von Luxemburg (1307-1354) im Jahre 1343 erbaut. Ihre gemauerten Bögen wurden auf die massiven Pfeiler der römischen Brücke aufgesetzt. Wie schon zuvor in römischer Zeit war auch diese neue Brücke durch Brückentore gesichert. Die Rekonstruktion, von Westen gesehen, zeigt die Tore auf den Flußpfeilern 2 und 7 (von Westen) und den Zugang zur Stadt auf dem stadtseitigen Brückenkopf, der in die Stadtbefestigung integriert war. Die Brückentore dienten neben der Sicherung und der Kontrolle der Zureisenden hauptsächlich der Zollerhebung. Im Jahre 1689 zerstörten die Franzosen diese Brücke, sie wurde dann unter Kurfürst Franz Ludwig (1716-1729) wieder hergestellt. Eine ältere Zeichnung von 1670 zeigt auf den Pfeilern 3 und 5 je zwei Säulen, ähnlich denen in römischer Zeit und an gleicher Stelle, die wohl der Signalgebung für die Schiffahrt dienten. Bei einem Häuschen auf Pfeiler 4 könnte es sich um ein Kapellchen des hl. Nikolaus, dem Patron der Schiffer, handeln, der auch heute noch auf der Südseite den Schiffern entgegenblickt.

The piers of this bridge are of Roman origin and date from the Roman Bridge built in the mid-2nd century. For about 1200 years, it presumably was the only fixed Moselle crossing between Metz in France and Coblenz. Its piers have borne all later bridges up to the present. The Roman bridges were wooden structures which rested on the stone piers. The first stone vaulting was constructed in 1343 under Archbishop Baldwin of Luxembourg (1307-1354). The masonry arches were set on the massive piers of the Roman Bridge. As in the Roman period, this new bridge was secured by bridge gates. The reconstruction, seen from the west, shows the gates on piers number 2 and 7 (counting from the west) and at the entry to the city on the city side of the bridge, with the gate integrated into the fortifications. The bridge gates served not only to secure the bridge and to control entry into the city but also to collect tolls. In 1689, French troops blew up this bridge, which was later restored under Elector Francis Louis (1716-1729). An older drawing from 1670 shows two columns each on piers number 3 and 5, similar to those in the same position in the Roman era, probably serving as signals for boat traffic. The small house on pier number 4 could be a chapel dedicated to the patron saint of sailors, St. Nicolas, who still greets boatmen on the south side of the bridge today.

Blick auf die Römerbrücke von Südwesten mit der barocken Einwölbung
View of the Roman Bridge from the southwest with the baroque vaulting

Kurfürst Franz Ludwig
Elector Francis Louis

Lambert Dahm 1996

Der Trierer Hafen um 1480
The Trier harbor in 1480

Der hier im Bildzentrum stehende Kran wurde 1413 im Auftrag des Schiffers Goebel und seiner Familie erbaut und auch betrieben. Nach deren Tod ging die Anlage vertragsgemäß in das Eigentum der Stadt über. Der rundum schwenkbare Kran konnte durch Treträder und Kettenwinden bedient werden und war für schwere Lasten bestimmt. Gegen Bezahlung konnten die Schiffe hier ent- und beladen werden. Er war bis 1910, also 500 Jahre, in Betrieb und hat redliche Dienste geleistet. Nach alten Unterlagen mußte er beispielsweise im Jahre 1524 alleine 2200 Fuder Wein bewegen. Die Stapelfläche zwischen Kaimauer und Stadtmauer war relativ groß, da die Stadtmauer einige Meter weiter östlich als die heutige Stützmauer des Straßendamms lag. Hier war der Hauptlandeplatz der Flußschiffe, deren Anlegestellen sich bis zur Römerbrücke hinzogen. Bereits in römischer Zeit legten hier die Schiffe an, allerdings lag der Hauptstapelplatz damals etwas weiter nördlich zu den Horrea (St. Irminen) hin. Hinter der Stadtmauer lag eines der Schifferwohnviertel, das durch die Johannispforte unmittelbar mit dem Hafen verbunden war. Die Johannispforte wurde später Krahnenpforte genannt. Das romantisch anmutende Bild sollte nicht darüber hinwegtäuschen, daß hier härteste Arbeit geleistet werden mußte. Neben der schweren körperlichen Beanspruchung waren die Schiffer wie auch die Hafenarbeiter fast ganzjährig jeder Witterung ausgesetzt.

In 1413, the crane seen in the center of the picture was commissioned, built, and subsequently operated by the boatman Goebel and his family. After their deaths, the facility came by contract into city ownership. Intended for heavy loads, the swivel-mounted roof with its loading booms could be operated by circular treadmills and wenches. Shippers paid to have their cargo loaded and unloaded here. The crane was in operation until 1910, 500 years, and rendered honest service. According to old records, in just the one year 1524, it had to move 2,200 casks of wine, each 240 gallons/960 liters. The loading and stacking area between the waterfront and the city wall was relatively large, as the wall was some yards/meters further to the east than the present-day high water embankment. This was the main landing stage for the river boats, with docking places stretching as far as the Roman Bridge. In the Roman era ships also docked here, but the main loading area at that time was somewhat further north near the Roman storehouses (St. Irmina's). The shippers' quarter was located behind the city wall, with the harbor directly accessible through St. John's Gate, later called Crane Gate. The picture's romantic atmosphere should not belie the back-breaking work done by these men. Besides the heavy physical labor, the shippers as well as the harbor laborers were exposed to all types of weather almost year round.

Moselkran am Radweg. Im Hintergrund die Römerbrücke
The Moselle crane on the cycling trail. Roman Bridge in the background

Heute ist der alte Kran durch Aufschüttungen von der Mosel getrennt
Today, the old crane is further from the Moselle because of landfill

Lambert Dahm 1997

Das Weberviertel mit dem Stadtbach um 1600

The weavers' quarter with the city brook around 1600

Dieses Bild gewährt einen Blick auf bürgerliches Leben und Wohnen in Trier. Die gezeigte Bebauung gehört zu dem durch das Handwerk geprägten Weberviertel. Es zog sich entlang des sogenannten Weberbachs und war hauptsächlich von Webern und Färbern bewohnt. Ihre Zunft war eine der bedeutendsten und reichsten der Stadt mit entsprechendem Einfluß. Das grüne Haus links war das Amtshaus der Wollfärber. Es wurde im 16. Jh. erbaut und "Haus zum Kronenbaum" genannt. Auffälligster Schmuck am Haus war ein Baum, der sehr geschickt über den Außenkamin hinweg gemalt war und in der Hauptgabelung eine vergoldete Adelskrone zeigte. Diese Krone sollte an eine kaiserliche Auszeichnung der Zunft erinnern, während der Baum an eine Tradition des Ortes erinnerte. Eine Reliefdarstellung am Amtshaus, hier ergänzt, bezog sich wahrscheinlich auf die Tätigkeit der Färber. Unmittelbar neben dem Amtshaus ging die Rahnengasse ab. In dem dritten Haus hinter der Rahnengasse befand sich zeitweise die jüdische Synagoge mit der Rabbinerwohnung. Der Weberbach, auch Stadtbach genannt, war eine Ableitung des Olewiger Baches und wurde bereits im 10. Jh. urkundlich erwähnt, er war nicht nur Grundlage für die beiden Textilgewerbe, er war für die ganze nördliche Stadt wichtig. Die Weber- und Färberhäuser gehörten bis zu ihrer Zerstörung im Zweiten Weltkrieg zu den wenigen erhaltenen gotischen Stadtvierteln innerhalb der deutschen Städte und hatten weit über Trier hinaus Bedeutung.

This picture permits a look into the life and living conditions of the Trier townspeople. The houses shown belong to the weavers' quarter, dominated by the skilled trades. It followed the path of the so-called Weavers' Brook and was inhabited primarily by weavers and dyers. Their guild was one of the most important and wealthiest in the city, with a corresponding amount of influence. The green house on the left was the guild house of the wool dyers. Built in the 16th century, it was named "House of the Crown Tree." The conspicuous ornament on the house was a tree painted cleverly over and around the exterior chimney and displaying a gilded nobleman's crown in the main tree fork. This crown was to commemorate an Imperial award to the guild, with the tree as a reminder of an old local tradition. A bas-relief on the house, drawn in full here, probably referred to the dyers' work. Rana's Lane (Rahnenstrasse) ran between the dyers' house and the neighboring house. For some time, the synagogue with the rabbi's dwelling was located in the third house beyond the entrance to Rana's Lane. Weavers' Brook, also simply city brook, was a branch of Olewig Brook and was documented as early as the 10th century. It was not only a fundamental element in both textile trades but was also vital for the entire medieval city. Until their destruction in World War II, the weavers' and dyers' houses belonged to the few preserved Gothic quarters in German cities and were of importance far beyond Trier.

Von den gotischen Häusern (vorne und nach rechts) ist nur noch der Verlauf des heute unter der Straße kanalisierten Weberbachs übrig
The canalized course of the Weavers' Brook under the street echoes the Gothic houses (foreground and to the right)

Lambert Dahm 1999

Literaturhinweise und Impressum
Further literature and Publisher

H&S Virtuelle Welten, Henerichs, Jörg (Hrsg. / ed.): Trier Die römische Stadt in Bildern / Trier The Roman City in Pictures. Verlag edition treverorum, Trier 2003.
H&S Virtuelle Welten, Henerichs, Jörg (Hrsg. / ed.): Stadtführer Erlebnis Trier / City Guide Experience Trier. Verlag edition treverorum, Trier 2002.
H&S Virtuelle Welten, Henerichs, Jörg (Hrsg. / ed.): CD-ROM Augusta Treverorum Treveris. Das römische Trier entdecken! / Discovering Roman Trier. Verlag edition treverorum, Trier 1998.

1 Gottfried Kentenich: Geschichte der Stadt Trier. Von ihrer Gründung bis zur Gegenwart. Trier 1915. Unveränderter Nachdruck: Akademische Buchhandlung Interbook, Trier 1979.
2 Hans Hubert Anton: Trier im Übergang von der römischen zur fränkischen Herrschaft, Francia 12 (1984).
3 Heinz Heinen: Frühchristliches Trier. Von den Anfängen bis zu Völkerwanderung. Paulinus-Verlag, Trier 1996.
4 Eugen Ewig: Trier im Merowingerreich, Civitas, Stadt, Bistum. Trierer Zeitschrift Jg. 21, 1952, Hrsg. Rheinisches Landesmuseum Trier.
5 Kurt Böhner: Die fränkischen Altertümer des Trierer Landes. Germ. Denkm. Völkerwanderungszeit Ser. B, 1, Berlin 1958.
6 Eugen Ewig: Das Trierer Land im Merowinger- und Karolingerreich, in: Richard Laufner (Hrsg.), Geschichte des Trierer Landes 1, (Schriftenreihe zur Trierischen Landesgeschichte und Volkskunde). Trier 1964.
7 Kurt Böhner: Das Trierer Land zur Merowingerzeit nach den Zeugnissen der Bodenfunde, in: Richard Laufner (Hrsg.), Geschichte des Trierer Landes 1, (Schriftenreihe zur Trierischen Landesgeschichte und Volkskunde 10) Trier 1964.
8 Lambert Dahm: Trier, Stadt und Leben im Mittelalter. Verlag der Akademischen Buchhandlung Interbook, Trier 1997.
9 Hubert Anton und Alfred Haverkamp: Trier im Mittelalter. 2000 Jahre Trier, Bd. 2, hrsg. von der Universität Trier. Spee-Verlag, Trier 1996.
10 Trier. Führer zu vor- und frühgeschichtlichen Denkmälern, 32, hrsg. vom Römisch-Germanischen Zentralmuseum Mainz. Verlag Philipp von Zabern, Mainz 1977.
11 G. Dehio, Handbuch der Deutschen Kunstdenkmäler, Rheinland- Pfalz, Saarland, bearbeitet von H. Caspary, W. Götz, E. Klinge. München-Berlin 1972.
12 Hermann Bunjes, Nikolaus Irsch, Gottfried Kentenich, Friedrich Kutzbach u. H. Lückger: Die kirchlichen Denkmäler der Stadt Trier. Mit Ausnahme des Domes, in: Die Kunstdenkmäler der Rheinprovinz, 13, 3. Abt. Düsseldorf 1938.
13 Adolf Neyses: Die Baugeschichte von St. Maximin in Trier; in: Die ehemalige Abteikirche St. Maximin in Trier, Geschichte, Renovierung, Umnutzung. Hrsg. vom Bischöfl. Generalvikariat Trier zur Eröffn. der wiederhergest. Maximinkirche am 25. Aug. 1995. Selbstverlag des Bischöfl. Dom-und Diözesanmuseums, Trier 1995.
14 Adolf Neyses: Die frühottonische Abteikirche St. Maximin in Trier; in: Kunstchronik 42 (1989), Heft 3, 102-109.
15 Adolf Neyses: Lage und Gestaltung von Grabinschriften im spätantiken Coemeterial-Großbau von St. Maximin in Trier; in: Jahrbuch des Römisch-Germanischen Zentralmuseums Mainz, 46 (1999), 413-446.
16 Theodor Konrad Kempf: Das Heiligtum des Bischofs und Märtyrers Paulinus in Trier. Pfarramt St. Paulin, Trier 1958.
17 Eberhard Zahn: Trier - Die Porta Nigra, die Simeonkirche, das Simeonstift. Rheinische Kunststätten, Hrsg. Rheinischer Verein für Denkmalpflege und Landschaftsschutz. Köln 1974.
18 Nikolaus Irsch: Der Dom zu Trier. Die Kunstdenkmäler der Rheinprovinz 13, 1. Trier 1938.
19 Theodor Konrad Kempf: Grundrißentwicklung und Baugeschichte des Trierer Domes. Der Dom zu Trier; in: Das Münster, Jg. 21, Heft 1 (1968).
20 Der Trierer Dom. Jahrbuch 1978/79, Rheinischer Verein für Denkmalpflege und Landschaftsschutz. Neuss 1980.
21 Winfried Weber: Der "Quadratbau" des Trierer Domes und sein polygonaler Einbau - Eine "Herrenmemoria"?; in: Der Heilige Rock zu Trier, Studien zur Geschichte und Verehrung der Tunika Christi. Paulinus-Verlag, Trier 1996.
22 Hans Eichler u. Richard Laufner: Hauptmarkt und Marktkreuz zu Trier. Eine kunst-, rechts- und wirtschaftsgeschichtliche Untersuchung. Trier 1958.
23 Lambert Dahm: Rekonstruktion der alten Brunnen im Bereich des Trierer Hauptmarktes um 1575; in: Neues Trierisches Jahrbuch (2003), 49-56.
24 Wolfgang Schmid: Der Petrusbrunnen auf dem Trierer Hauptmarkt. Ein Werk Hans Ruprecht Hoffmanns von 1595. Trier 1995.
25 Eberhard Zahn: Die Basilika in Trier. Römisches Palatium - Kirche zum Erlöser, Schriftenreihe des Rheinischen Landesmuseums, Nr. 6 (1991), hrsg. von der Evangelischen Kirchengemeinde Trier.
26 Eberhard Zahn: Der kurfürstliche Palast in Trier. Rheinische Kunststätten, Heft 103, Hrsg. Verein für Denkmalpflege und Landschaftsschutz, 3. Aufl. Köln 1982.
27 Theresia Zimmer: Das Kloster St. Irminen-Oeren in Trier von seinen Anfängen bis ins 13. Jahrhundert; in: Trierer Zeitschrift, Jg. 23 (1954/1955), Hrsg. Rheinisches Landesmuseum Trier.
28 Kurt Böhner: Die Anfänge der ehemaligen Abteikirche St. Martin zu Trier; in: Trierer Zeitschrift, Jg. 18 (1949), Hrsg. Rheinisches Landesmuseum Trier.
29 Nikolaus Irsch: St. Matthias zu Trier und die Trierisch-Lothringische Bautengruppe (1927).
30 St. Matthias zu Trier. Festschrift zum 30. April 1967.
31 Petrus Becker: Die Benediktinerabtei Sankt Eucharius- Sankt Matthias vor Trier. Germania Sacra N.F., 34,8. Berlin, New York 1996.

Verlag / Publisher:
H&S Virtuelle Welten GmbH
Heinrich-Weitz-Str. 8 - 54295 Trier
Tel.: +49 (0) 6 51 / 9 94 01 69
Fax: +49 (0) 6 51 / 4 29 35
Internet:www.virtuelle-welten.tv
Email: info@virtuelle-welten.tv
© 2004 H&S Virtuelle Welten GmbH, Trier
ISBN: 3-935313-04-7
1. Auflage November 2004 / 1st Printing November 2004

Herausgeber / Publisher: Jörg Henerichs
Zeichner und Autor / Texts and Drawings: Lambert Dahm
Redaktion / Editorial staff: H&S Virtuelle Welten GmbH
Englische Übersetzung / English translation:
Frankie und / and Hans-Joachim Kann
Gestaltung, Bildbearbeitung, Satz & Layout /
Design, picture processing, setting & layout: H&S Virtuelle Welten GmbH

Bildnachweis / Picture credits:
l = links / left, r = rechts / right, o = oben / top, m = mitte / center, u = unten / bottom, U = Umschlag / jacket, S. = Seite / page
Rheinisches Landesmuseum Trier / (Archaeological Museum): S. 3, 4, 5, 6u, 8o, 9o, 10m, 11u, 38l, 38m, 38r, 42l, 42r, 44l, 44m; Carl Stenz -Die Trierer Kurfürsten: S. 6o, 7l, 7r, 8u, 9l, 9m, 9r, 11o, 12, H&S Virtuelle Welten GmbH: S. 54m, 74l, 94r, 96r, 98r, 100r; Jörg Henerichs: S. U1l, U1m, U2, U3, U4l, U4o, 16, 20, 24, 30, 32, 40, 50l, 50r, 52, 56, 58r, 62r, 64, 68, 76, 82, 86l, 86r, 90, 92l, 92r, 98l, 100l; Gerhard Steinle: S. 22, 34, 36, 46, 48, 54l, 58l, 60, 62l, 66, 70, 74r, 78, 80, 84l, 88, 94l, 96l, 102; Svea Longen: S. U1r, 72, 84r; Dr. Karl-Josef Gilles: S. 10o; Stadtbibliothek Trier: S. 10u